P9-CBS-539

present
moments

present moments

Cherishing Everyday Experiences

A BOOK OF REFLECTIONS

stephen m. miller

SERVANT PUBLICATIONS
ANN ARBOR, MICHIGAN

© 1999 by Stephen M. Miller
All rights reserved.

Vine Books is an imprint of Servant Publications especially designed to serve
evangelical Christians.

All Scripture quotations, unless otherwise indicated, are taken from *The Holy
Bible, New International Version*®. © 1973, 1978, 1984 by the International
Bible Society. Used by permission of Zondervan Publishing House. All rights
reserved.

Servant Publications
P.O. Box 8617
Ann Arbor, Michigan 48107

Cover photograph: © Michael Keller/The Stock Market. Used by permission.

99 00 01 02   10 9 8 7 6 5 4 3 2 1

Printed in the United States of America

ISBN 1-56955-055-7

LIBRARY OF CONGRESS CATALOGING-IN-PUBLICATION DATA

Miller, Steve, 1952-
   Present moments : cherishing everyday experiences / Stephen M. Miller.
     p. cm.
   ISBN 1-56955-055-7 (alk. paper)
   1. Christian life. I. Title.
BV4501.2.M496   1999
248.2—dc21   99-11113
                                           CIP

c o n t e n t s

CHAPTER 1

The Moment of Discovery

We were born only yesterday.
JOB 8:9

A most unlikely scene changed the way I'd been living my life. And the person with the starring role never knew she had done a thing.

I was in my garage, wiping wax off the family Ford. My two children had helped me apply the wax, probably because it looked like a messy job. I rewarded them with Popsicles; Bradley, then age four, took his and meandered off to play. Rebecca, almost seven, stayed behind. As I buffed the car with an old towel, I glanced over at her sitting on a toy four-wheeler parked about six feet away. She was in a bit of a daze, perhaps daydreaming or recovering from her work on this warm spring afternoon.

I had nothing to do with the thought that came to me then. It felt like a mental invasion, an awareness poured into me by someone else.

She's nearly halfway gone from your home.

I stopped mid-stroke, frozen in that instant of awareness.

When painful emotion grips me, it usually does so by the throat, choking into a whisper any words I try to speak. I said, "Rebecca, I love you." But she didn't hear me, and was quickly on her way.

Barring tragedy, I would have her in my daily life another ten years or so. But if those years passed as quickly as the previous ones, my daughter would be gone in a moment. For it was just a moment ago that I made her acquaintance in a Kansas hospital delivery room, taught her how to ride a bike, and chauffeured her to her first day of kindergarten—while her mom sat beside me and cried.

Life Before the Discovery

I remember when life never seemed to change much.

I can still picture myself, a gangling squirt of a kid, lying on Grandma Miller's porch swing. Grandpa had built the swing in his tiny blacksmith shop near the barn. But I thought of it as Grandma's swing because it was she who made it such a delightful place to rest. She had sewn for it a billowy, inch-thick cushion that she placed on the seat each morning and removed each evening.

In this memory I lay in the shape of a comma, with my head on the left arm rest, my back on the cushion, and my feet propped against the string of chain shaped like an upside down Υ that rose from the right arm rest and gripped a hook in the ceiling. Gently I pumped the legs of the Υ with my feet, nudging the swing left and right instead of forward and backward. From this swaying perch on a rounded hilltop in West Virginia, my eyes traced the half-mile dirt driveway that dipped into the small valley (which we called "the holler") and then swooped back up a gently sloping hill where my grandparents' only cow and horse grazed near the one-lane gravel road just past the eastern fence line. Beyond the hill and the dusty road, and above the treetops bowing to the wind, the purple ridges of the Appalachian mountains rose like spikes on a dinosaur's back.

It was a beautiful scene I had enjoyed all of my young life.

I never consciously thought, "This will be forever." I just never realized it would one day end.

Every summer and many weekends throughout the year, Dad and Mom would bring our family here, from our Ohio home two hundred miles away. My two brothers, two sisters, and I would jump in the hayloft whenever we pleased. In the early morning, when dew soaks the shoes and pant legs of children, I would follow Grandpa into the musty, wooded valley to check his box rabbit traps. Between meals I would eat Grandma's pumpkin pie, made from pumpkins she grew. Sometimes I would sit on the porch with her, snapping and stringing green beans in the afternoon shade. When my family's summer vacation merged with those of aunts and uncles, I got to play with cousins I never saw but there. Francis and Guy, near my own age, were among my favorites.

Then, late one October, Grandpa died.

Grandma sold the farm and moved to Alabama with her daughter's family. I never saw Francis or Guy again. Grandma often wrote me, but I saw her only a couple of times in the decade longer that she lived. The people who bought the farm tore down the porch and pounded "No Trespassing" signs into the hilltop.

You've probably had shattering experiences like this, when

happy reality disintegrated. If you're like me, it didn't make much difference in the way you lived afterward. You still took for granted the cherished people and circumstances remaining in your life. You treated them no differently than before. You just learned to live with the uneasy awareness that the scenery could change.

I find it strange that God didn't use a crisis or a traumatic twist of fate to convince me life is fleeting—"swifter than a weaver's shuttle" and "but a breath," as the ailing and reflective Job put it. God could also have delivered this insight at the dawn of a new stage in my life. For instance, he had what seems a perfect opportunity when I started working part-time to save money for college, and suddenly found myself home alone at vacation time.

I did realize, with sadness, that my vacations with Dad and Mom and my brothers and sisters were over. No more camping in the Florida Keys, or chasing watermelons that escaped from the tiny rock harbor we built on the banks of a Colorado mountain stream. This end to my family vacations didn't make me noticeably more aware of the swiftness of life. Perhaps it became a tiny step toward the discovery. But I didn't begin treating my family, friends, job, or school as though they were treasures I'd one day have to leave behind. It didn't occur to me to embrace and enjoy them while they were still within my reach. They were part of the changing scenery, but my eyes were fixed on the road ahead. I had no time to dwell on the here and now. I was headed for the then and there.

To deliver his message, God chose a little girl who said nothing.

Physical Time Isn't Like
Spiritual Time

Only after I realized how soon my daughter would be gone from my daily life did I begin to understand what Peter meant when he wrote, "With the Lord ... a thousand years are like a day" (2 Peter 3:8). I used to read that verse and think, *Come on. Anyone with a snapping synapse could see through this attempt to explain away the apostles' earlier teaching that Jesus would return soon. After thirty years or more of no-show, you redefine "soon."*

But the fact is, there are two ways to measure time.

In physical time, measured by the calendar, Rebecca's good-bye in about ten years could seem so far down the pike that I figure I have all the time in the world to play with her, teach her, and show her how important she is to me. I might even begin to think of her as a burden parked on my shoulders and growing heavier with each Happy Meal. Instead of cherishing our time together, I could actually start thinking of her as a cross I have to bear.

In soul time, the fleeting sense of which we experience only in hindsight, Rebecca's good-bye is as near as my next breath. "Life," says the psalmist, agreeing with Job, "is but a breath" (39:5). One of Job's counselors adds that we were born yesterday (see 8:9).

There's nothing distorted or artificially compressed about soul time, experienced in the backward look. It's real. Ask folks who have lived long enough to look back on their memories of decades ago. Does the time seem like years? Or does it seem like moments?

To Dr. Mary Scott, a missionary friend of mine who died recently at age eighty-seven, her internment in a Japanese prisoner of war camp more than fifty calendar years ago was not a distant recollection. When she spoke of it, she wept. The memory was fresh, the detail vivid, the emotion fully preserved.

To Dr. Ralph Earle, chairman of the committee of scholars that translated the New International Version of the Bible, his marriage to Mabel seemed like a recent event. Yet their white hair, weathered skin, and trembling hands confirmed that according to calendar time, they had been married sixty-three years. They attended the same church I did, and I rarely saw one without the other. After Mabel died on March 15, 1995, Ralph followed two months later. Without Mabel, perhaps Ralph experienced the other half of Peter's phrase about soul time: "With the Lord a day is like a thousand years." In time measured by the soul, one sad day can seem that long.

Though the calendar years pile up, soul time seems absolutely unaffected and unconnected to this physical measurement. Wilfrid Sheed, an author in his late sixties and a survivor of polio and cancer, observes, "No one ever told me how little you change inside. One's twelve-year-old self and one's present self feel exactly the same."

I know what he means. I remember one night tucking my children in bed, after a couple rounds of wrestling them on the living room floor. From beneath the covers Rebecca, still in elementary school, looked up at me and asked, "Daddy, why do you play so much?"

"Because," I said, "I'm just a little boy in a grown man's body."

She chuckled, certain I was kidding.

I wasn't.

My childhood ended almost thirty calendar years ago. But in the heart and memory of my soul, my childhood seems like a few seconds ago. Nevertheless, my childhood is gone. I can no longer climb King Kong rock with my little brother and swing from the steel cable that dangled from the stout limb of an adjacent monster tree. The rock and tree disappeared when the Rolling Acres Mall arrived. And my little brother is now bigger than I am.

Yet the nearness of those days is more authentic than the stack of calendars conveys.

How the Discovery Changes Us

When we discover how fleeting life is—when the reality plunges its roots deep into our mind and our emotion—we become new creatures. We start seeing things differently. Our attitudes change, and so do our actions.

Once, for example, my then eight-year-old son and I were standing along the inside wall of the school gymnasium, watching his sister and her classmates serenade a packed house of video-recording parents. Bradley couldn't see his former teacher playing the piano, so without asking his permission I reached down to pick him up. Early in his life I had trained him to help out my aging back by jumping to the rhythm of my lift. And he always jumped. Until this moment.

I was standing behind him and to his right, with my hands positioned as arches cradled beneath his armpits. I sent the message to jump by pulling slightly downward, as though tensing a spring. But the instant we had liftoff, I could tell that not all rockets were firing. His arms hung limp at his side and his weight was that of a dead astronaut. He wasn't helping at all. I, however, was committed to the lift partly because I didn't want to look like a wimp in front of the folks standing near me.

When I returned him to the hardwood floor and leaned over to ask him if he saw the teacher, all he said was, "That was embarrassing."

I apologized, then stood silently beside him with my hand on his shoulder, realizing what his words and body language had told me. A year earlier he had used both of these to ask me to stop kissing him good-bye in front of his schoolmates. And now, he was telling me that my time for lifting him in public was over. Too soon he will not want me putting my arm around him when others are watching. So I will cherish my hand on his shoulder for as long as he lets me rest it there.

That's how the discovery changes us. We realize that there are moments of opportunity that will come and go more quickly than a child can say, "Pick me up, Daddy." And we embrace what we would otherwise overlook, delay, or push aside. We arrive from work to a home littered with marbles, dolls, and coloring books and the children playing vigorously, recognizing that this is our messy moment when a neat house is less important than a fun house. Someday the clutter will be gone, we remind ourselves, but so will the children.

We find a private moment with our own aging father to stumble and fumble yet somehow deliver the feelings we've long held but never expressed in words: "I love you, Dad."

And as his eyes fill, ours do the same. We find patience for temperamental kin who come for the holidays, because we realize that this is one of our few moments together and that differences need not consume our moment.

Moving Past Our Regrets

Once we discover how quickly life is passing, we not only begin to cherish the fleeting moments as they come, we begin to regret those that got away.

There is a herd of social psychologists who specialize in studying regret; they conduct ongoing research to find out what we humans regret most and how we cope with those regrets. I've talked with half a dozen of these specialists, and I've learned that if they could sit down with each one of us and talk as friend to friend, they'd make sure we understood at least two things.

Regret Is Good
If we regret something, like hurting our family, that means we care enough to be sorry. The trouble is that people in our culture—though not in every culture—hate negative emotions. So instead of thinking about our regrets and lingering with them long enough to learn from them, we bury them, ignore them, or deny they ever existed. We say we have no regrets—at least none worth mentioning.

Dr. Janet Landman, a Babson College professor of psychology, told me, "I can't imagine anyone living into adulthood and not making a mistake that they care about. If you make a mistake and you care about it, then regret is the emotional consequence."

Regret is good in the same way that physical pain is good. It's a warning. It's a clue that something is wrong and we'd better look into it. A sixty-four-year-old grandmother in Dallas told me, however, "Regret is a waste of time. Dwelling on the past limits your future." Reseachers disagree. They say the opposite is true.

Landman, for instance, told me of a woman in her sixties who couldn't acknowledge regret. "This woman has lived her entire adult life with an abusive husband," Landman said. "She can't leave the house without his permission. She has to beg him for every penny. She's not allowed to eat out, but he eats out whenever he wants to. It would be hard for her to say, 'I made a huge mistake, and because of it most of my life has been miserable.' But if she could, her next twenty years might not be that way, even if her previous forty are ruined."

Studies show that we can reduce our regrets in the future by remembering our regrets in the past. Part of the reason for this is because regret is an emotion that prods us to act. It pesters us to apologize and to make things right. And it warns us of similar problems ahead.

One big reason some folks do nothing about past mistakes is because they're ashamed. Regret mobilizes, but shame paralyzes. Shame makes us want to drop into a hole or turn invisible.

Bank robber Katherine Ann Power hid for twenty-three years before regret managed to overcome her sense of shame. She was a Brandeis University senior and part of an anti-Vietnam War group that tried to launch a revolution to stop what she felt was an unjust war. To fund the revolution, the group decided to "liberate" money from "the establishment" that condoned the war. Power drove the switch car the day they robbed a bank outside of Boston. She said she learned several hours after the robbery—to her horror—that one of the gunmen had shot and killed a police officer. The policeman had nine children.

Power moved across the continent, to Oregon, took on a new identity, married, raised a family, became a restaurant consultant and cooking teacher, and volunteered her time for charitable causes—all the while remaining on the FBI's "10 Most Wanted" list longer than any other woman in history. On the day she turned herself in, September 15, 1993, she pleaded guilty to manslaughter—though the district attorney said that without her guilty plea he would not have had enough evidence to convict her. Three weeks later she was sentenced to eight years in prison and twenty years probation.

Regret is good not only because it pushes us to do the right thing, it preserves our integrity and decency. If we care enough to regret, that means we're holding fast to our highest values, in spite of our stumbling. We may have hurt someone, but if we regret it, we still value them.

Let Go of Regrets You Can't Undo
This is the second piece of advice the psychologist researchers would offer us. Go ahead and identify the biggest regrets in your life, they'd say. Spend time thinking about them, make restitution if you can, and promise yourself not to make the same mistakes again. But don't beat yourself up over something you can't change.

Dr. Tom Gilovich, social psychologist at Cornell University, says people need to realize that as the years go by, regret has a way of growing—instead of diminishing. This is especially true of regrets over missed opportunities. He says warped hindsight is partly to blame.

"When people look back on what they should have done," says Gilovich, "they're looking through rose-colored glasses and misrepresenting the probabilities of success." If people could realize how common this is, he said, they'd more easily let go of these regrets.

Cherishing the Present Moment

The time spent with our regrets—before releasing them into the redeeming hands of God—is time well invested. It's one thing to know in our brain that the present moment is already slipping through our fingers. It's another to know it in our heart because we've felt the pain of a moment missed.

I regret working as much as I did as a teenager. Nearly every weeknight after school and each weekend I pumped gas at a filling station to pay for my clunky set of wheels and to save for college. I missed my moment to concentrate on my studies and to enjoy after-school sports and clubs. I settled for a bunch of Bs, a few As, and one measly season of track during junior high. That regret, known in my brain and felt in my heart, is affecting the way I'm raising my kids.

As I write this, Bradley has discovered karate (and is quite capable of inflicting wrenching spasms on my solar plexus). He's also finishing his third season of baseball, and is anticipating his ninth season of soccer and his third season of basketball. Rebecca is now making pleasing sounds on the piano (after all those lessons), and she's been through three seasons of basketball and her first season of volleyball. This is their moment to experiment with hobbies, skills, and more fun than you can shake a stick at. And it's my moment to help them.

I could have heard this in a parenting seminar, believed it in my head, and failed to act on it because I assigned it a low priority. Instead, I discovered it by lingering with my regrets. Then I experienced it in my heart and assigned it a priority worthy of my time. I don't know what kind of dividends it will pay, other than the shelf of trophies we already have and enough team uniforms to open up a used sports clothing outlet. But if one of the studies at Cornell University is correct, it won't pay off in regrets. Not one person expressed regret over a hobby they had learned—even if they had long since abandoned it. The new skill left them with an enduring sense of accomplishment.

"There is a time for everything," says the sage of Ecclesiastes, "and a season for every activity under heaven" (3:1).

There is a time to embrace and a time to push aside, he says. Unfortunately, he doesn't say when to do which.

One great clue lies in the discovery that life is but a moment, in time measured by the spirit. Once we realize this, we begin to embrace the people and the opportunities that only briefly pass our way. And we try to help others do the same.

CHAPTER 2

A Moment for Childhood

Jesus ... took the children in his arms,
put his hands on them and blessed them.
MARK 10:14, 16

B radley was barely three years old when he stumbled, bug-eyed and crying, into the living room where I was reading. When I asked what was wrong, he said his sister, then five, had jumped on his stomach while they were playing in the backyard.

I carried Bradley outside and called Rebecca over, asking her to sit on top of the picnic table so I could talk to her.

"Bradley came into the house crying," I told her. "What made him cry?"

Rebecca's head gyrated left and right, then up and down, as though she were trying to work loose an idea. Her eyes searched about, and her hands toyed with her face. Finally she spoke. I remember her words exactly because I wrote them on a pad of paper shortly after she spoke them.

"God made my thinking very bad. And you know what he made me think? Jump on Bradley's tummy!" She stomped her feet on the seat of the picnic table, to punctuate her point, I suppose.

I'm afraid I let a smile crack through. I know I shouldn't have. But sometimes it's matter over mind. Quickly, I told her to sit in time-out—five minutes of playless prison. Afterward I gave her a short, age-adjusted lesson in theology: God does not make us do bad things.

Tummy trampoline has been just one of many skirmishes between my kids. Since then they've engaged one another in yelling, biting, slapping, kicking, hair pulling, and gobbling up the other's treat. This isn't the normal fare around our household; the kids can go for days without exchanging a cross word or tattling a tale. Most of the time, in fact, they live at peace with one another and seem to enjoy each other's company.

May it be even more so in the days ahead. It's my job, I believe, to help make this happen. My youngest sister, Pam, feels the same way about the responsibility she has for her grade-school son and her preschool daughter. Whenever the two start bickering, she tells them, "Be kind and loving." She repeats this phrase enough that she says she has thought of putting it on cassette tape so all she has to do is push a button when her kids need the reminder. In fact, she repeats the phrase enough, says her husband, that when she dies he wants someone to write on her gravestone, "She was kind and loving."

My sister and I are taking our cue from the wise writer of Proverbs, who sounds like an experienced family man. He said, "Better a dry crust with peace and quiet than a house full of feasting, with strife" (17:1). Jesus, who grew up with brothers and sisters, also knew a thing or two about life on the home front—enough that when he sent his seventy-two followers on a healing and preaching mission into the villages, he gave them these first words to speak when entering a home: "Peace to this house" (Luke 10:5). That was a common greeting, probably because it was a common need. Just about any household with kids—and ancient families preferred lots of kids to help with the work—is a house of chaos in need of peace.

It's not just for my sake that I want my kids to get along with each other and to enjoy their childhood together, though their getting along certainly brightens my life. It's for their own sake and for the loving, lifelong relationship that I want the two of them to experience.

Sometimes when Rebecca and Bradley are arguing over what seems, judging by their behavior, essential to planetary survival—such as who gets the TV remote control or the last Fruit Roll-Up—I think about my brothers and sisters. The thoughts and feelings that spring up are ones I wish I could mind-meld into my children, the way Spock of "Star Trek" communicated brain to brain with a wide array of uncooperative creatures.

Instead, I use mere words that, I sometimes fear, do little more than bounce off eardrums. "You're not going to be living together a whole lot longer," I tell them. "In fact, your time together in the same house is more than half over."

"Good!" That's what they say. And in the beet-red flush of anger, that's exactly what they feel.

But that's not what I want them to feel.

"Uncle Cliff, Uncle Darb (short for Darwin), Aunt Louise, and Aunt Pam are my brothers and sisters," I've reminded them. "I used to live with them. Cliff and Darb and I slept in the same room. But now they all live eight hundred miles away from me, and I'm lucky if I get to see them once a year. I miss them a lot." My family stayed in the Akron, Ohio, area, where Mom and Dad raised us, but I moved to Kansas City to attend seminary and then decided to stay.

Rebecca and Bradley know that what I say is true because they complain that they don't get to play with their cousins enough. But I'm almost certain they don't understand what all of this has to do with their relationship to each other. They have fully functioning imaginations, yet I'm sure they can't begin to imagine life apart from one another. But I, in those times of homesickness that have never completely gone away, have to muscle my memory in order to wring from it everything I can about what it was like to live with my brothers and sisters.

Feuding Kids

We sometimes argued and fought when I was growing up. Once I hand-scooped the mashed potatoes off my little brother Darb's dinner plate and shoved them up his nose. We were all aghast, myself included, for I had never done anything like that, before or since. I don't remember what Darb had said to warrant the nose mashing. But I do remember his surprising reaction. After a tense pause, he started to laugh. Everyone followed suit, to my great relief, because this act was so uncharacteristic of me.

I prefer to think that T. Berry Brazelton, retired professor of pediatrics at Harvard Medical School, is right: youthful family fights like ours simply fuel our passionate relationships. Brazelton said he became worried when his own daughters, at ages six and four, were constantly teasing and fighting each other. But one night he overheard the older girl hatching a plot with her little sister. The tiny plotter knew where Daddy hid the candy, and she would snatch some for both girls if Sis stood lookout. Brazelton said he didn't take it personally, since he saw in the scheme evidence that his daughters were becoming devoted to one another.

In my household, we five Miller kids teased, taunted, and ridiculed each other up one day and down the next. Yet, we too developed an enduring devotion to one another.

While walking home from grade school together one spring day, Darb flipped off one of his shoes and threw it from a small bridge into the middle of the creek near our house. This creek is called Mud Run, for good reason. Home to leeches, snails, and zigzagging snakes, the water flowed above a thick and slippery bed of sedentary slime.

Walking with us was our next-door neighbor, a boy about a year older than I. Our neighbor promptly came up with an idea for retrieving the shoe. He would hold me by my ankles, suspending me upside down from the railing along the side of the bridge. As I dangled above the water, I would pluck up the shoe. He said he was sure he could hold me.

And he did hold me. For three or four seconds.

Then he announced that I was slipping—as though I hadn't noticed my head bobbing perilously closer to the water a few inches below. He held on for another second or two, then I was gone with a splash. I performed a momentary but amazing handstand in about three inches of water and three inches of muck. As I tumbled slowly over onto my back and lay for an instant with the leeches, I gave no thought to my brother's shoe. My single consideration was to get vertical—right side up this time—and to slosh my way out of the sludge. As I stood on the bank and checked my body for disgusting creatures, my friend asked why I didn't pick up the shoe on my way out.

Good question, for a dry guy. I eventually retrieved Darb's shoe the way I should have in the first place, with a long pole from our garage.

I didn't know it then, but my willingness to dangle over the side of a bridge on my brother's behalf was just one of many evidences of the devotion that the Miller kids developed for each other. Team Miller stared down solitary bullies who hadn't learned that you couldn't fight just one Miller. We defended each other against insults from outsiders, though maintaining full right to insult from within. And when one of us was in trouble or overwhelmed, we became a swarm of support.

When I wrecked my bike on Suicide Hill, producing road rash scars I'm still wearing thirty-five years later and twisting my front bike tire into an abstract geometric figure that would not roll, my little brother Cliff tried to carry my busted bike the half-mile home. When it proved too heavy for him, he raced to our house to get the family. They all came running to my rescue through the blueberry patch: Mom at the front, Granny at the tail, and the kids in between (Dad was working).

Decades have passed, though they seem a swift blur. We Miller kids each have our own families now, and we run in different circles. Even the Akron gang will sometimes go months without seeing each other. Yet inexplicably the devotion seems steadfast, timeless, powerful, and occasionally irrational because it's so unconditional.

When Darb ended up in jail as a suspect in a crime, we didn't ask if he was guilty. In the moment of crisis when our mother called each one of us, we asked what the bail was, and those who had money sent it. Guilty or not (he was not), we didn't want our brother behind bars if we had the right and the resources to set him free.

When the Feuding Never Stops

Family relationships don't always work out this well. Unfortunately, as the sage of Proverbs observed, "An offended brother is more unyielding than a fortified city, and disputes are like the barred gates of a citadel" (18:19).

When family feuds cut too deep and fester too long, devotion and love can die. I don't know what drove the wedge between my Grandpap Williams and his older brother. Mom and others say the two probably wouldn't have known themselves, but Mom suspects the problem sprang from their growing-up years. Both were strong-minded. And my grandfather was a change-of-life baby, the youngest of six, and one who grew up feeling like he was just an extra mouth to feed, especially since he was only three years old when his father died.

My mom remembers the bitter separation between these two brothers clear back to when she was a wisp of a preschooler. After Grandpap's father died, the family's hilly, tree-dense West Virginia homestead was divided among the children. Grandpap got eighteen slanting acres and the old wooden farmhouse; his mom lived with him. Grandpap's older brother lived in a house a few hundred yards away, down the curved dirt lane, across the shallow bedrock creek, and hidden behind a narrow forest wall of pine, black walnut, oak, and sassafras.

Grandpap opened a sawmill business before the Great

Depression, but when the nation's finances crashed and people stopped buying lumber, Grandpap's partner stole what cash the sawmill had and fled the state. Grandpap was known for his near-obsessive honesty; he was determined to pay off his business debts. So he borrowed money from one of his sisters, who tried unsuccessfully to convince him to accept the money as a gift. The pressures of paying back his sister while trying to feed his family of four children, a wife, and a mother proved more than he could handle. Overwhelmed, my grandfather plunged into a private great depression. Hearing of this, Grandpap's brother—a friend of the municipal judge—reported Grandpap's condition to the judge, who ordered a hearing and then committed my grandfather to an insane asylum.

In those days the sheriff came to arrest such people, locking them in the local jail for the night before starting the daylong drive to the facility in Weston. Grandpap, a proud man, didn't want his family to see him arrested. So he walked into town, about ten miles away.

Mom, who was only three years old at the time, says she remembers the heart-ripping scene when he left. Grandpap loved cooked prunes. So his mother fixed him a bowl to eat before he began the long, solitary walk into town. For some reason that my mom can't explain, Grandpap's mother didn't hand him the bowl. Instead, she spoon-fed him, just as she had done when he was a little boy. As he ate the fruit, he began to sob. And soon he was gone.

On the Sundays that followed, my mom remembers her mother taking all the children to play in the creek, a quarter mile downstream. This was to get away from visitors who came "asking questions."

Nine months later, Grandpap was released. He had a little coal on some property nearby, so he decided to dig it and sell what he could. Unfortunately, he had to walk past his brother's house to get to the tiny mine. All too often, on Grandpap's way home from work in the evening, his brother would come outside and taunt him.

My grandmother knew this, so when my mom was five years old she was given the daily task of going to the mine to get Grandpap so he wouldn't have to walk home alone. On her way there, she ran past her uncle's house. When she reached the head of the mine she called for her daddy. On their walk home, my mom held Grandpap's sooty hand, positioning herself between her uncle's house and her father.

As the pair approached the house, Grandpap's brother would come outside to the front porch, prop a foot up on the banister, and begin cleaning his pipe. Then he'd ask, "Heard from Judge Wilhelm lately, Charlie?" Judge Wilhelm was the municipal judge who had committed him.

Grandpap had already told his skinny little red-haired daughter what to do: "Speak and go on." The two would wave, say hello, and continue walking.

I'd like to think that I inherited a heart big enough to respond the same way my grandfather did. In spite of years of mistreatment by his big brother, Grandpap was keeping the door open for reconciliation. Unfortunately, there would be none.

The mangled feelings that destroyed the relationship between Grandpap and his brother survived along family lines for generations, partly because Grandpap's kids grew up amid ridicule about having a father who was sent to the "crazy house." Not many years ago, Grandpap's son, who had inherited the eighteen acres, died. The land went to his widow, my aunt. Perhaps some day her sons, my cousins, will own the property.

But at my uncle's funeral, a grandson of Grandpap's brother reportedly asked my young cousins who owned the property now. This question set off a firestorm. That's because years earlier another member of this family had asked my uncle to sell him the land so the original family tract could be reunited. But my uncle had refused to sell it into the family that had caused his dad such grief.

The relatives remained polite at the funeral, but afterward, when word got around about the query—and the timing of it—there erupted an explosion of angry letters, high-decibel phone calls, and attempts at apologies judged insincere. Members of both families have since been trying to heal the shredded relationships, but it's hard. The psalmist was right: an offended brother—or cousin, or uncle, or any other relative—can be "more unyielding than a fortified city."

This is but a snapshot of what happens when the moment of childhood is twisted, distorted, and horribly damaged, turning loved ones into despised ones. We parents need to explore ways to help our children "be kind and loving," as my younger sister puts it. If the children are beginning to develop a sense of how quickly the summer vacation ended or how swiftly the school year has passed, perhaps we can use this emerging awareness to alert them that their days as children living together will, in much the same way, come to an end too soon. And we can tell them that one of the greatest gifts they can give us is this: in the years ahead, when they're thinking back on the time they spent with their brothers and sisters, that they remember scenes of kindness and love.

You don't have to be a parent to deliver this short lecture. I did it a few weeks ago—to a kid in someone else's family. We were spending the day with that family, which has two teenage boys, and we decided to play a little baseball. During the game the older boy began tossing verbal barbs at his brother, a teammate who was trying to pitch but having a hard time getting the ball across the plate: "You fat bum. You can't even pitch a ball." There was no anger in his tone; he spoke matter-of-factly, which I found all the more disturbing. I replied in a kidding, gently chiding tone, but with words I fiercely believe: "He's your brother. Be supportive. You're not supposed to hurt him." After about two more exchanges like this, the older teenager seemed to get my message, and he stopped badgering his brother. At least while I was around.

I know that child-rearing experts say that kids need to learn to solve their own problems and that by learning to assert themselves, defend themselves, and compromise, they develop social skills that will help them survive in the adult world. But letting kids work out their own problems shouldn't mean no holds barred. If harm begins—either by words or actions—grown-ups need to step in.

If we're a parent with grown children who don't get along, or if we're estranged from one of our own brothers or sisters, we can gently lobby for reconciliation. The dying wish of Jacob was for the reconciliation of his sons. Several of his sons had sold their brother Joseph to slave traders, who took him to Egypt. In Egypt, Joseph rose to a powerful position which gave him the authority to get revenge. But as Joseph's father lay dying he asked that this message be delivered to his privileged son: "I ask you to forgive your brothers the sins and the wrongs they committed in treating you so badly" (Genesis

50:17). When Joseph heard this, he wept. Then he did something that would not surprise the youngsters in my little sister's house. Joseph told his brothers he forgave them "and spoke kindly to them" (v. 21).

Raising Kids Who Love Each Other

How do we raise kids who love each other when they're young, so they'll love each other when they're grown?

As long as God gives people the freedom to make their own choices—for better or worse—there will be no such thing as a foolproof strategy. But I'd like to think we can influence the choices of others, pointing them toward love and, when necessary, showing them the way to reconciliation.

Shared Experiences

My brothers and sisters and I are bound by a childhood of shared adventures, joys, and sorrows. We remember and still talk about vacations spent sleeping eight in a camper built for four (Granny came with us). We remember helping Mom buff the freshly waxed dining room floor by skating across it in our socks.

We also remember the Saturday night when Mom washed out the last of Dad's hair, a side effect of his chemotherapy. When Dad stepped into the living room, where we waited, he spoke with a single, startling question: "Do you still love me?" Not one who typically expressed his deepest feelings, Dad had never asked us that before. We loved him, but I can't remember ever speaking of it until that night.

Expressed Feelings

One day I sat on our front steps and watched a neighbor across the street pull her giggling, waving little girls in a red wagon, up and down her driveway. After my neighbor had pulled for a minute or two, I noticed that she raised her left arm and looked at her wristwatch. Time was getting away, she must have thought. So she pulled the wagon into the garage, unloaded the kids, and went back into the house.

In that moment when she looked at her watch, a wave of emotion rushed through me. I had been watching her as a reflection of my own past: what seemed just a few ticks of the clock ago I was pulling my two children in their red wagon as they giggled in delight and waved to anyone and everyone who happened by. The scene I was witnessing looked like a living parable, a symbolic yet vividly clear story of what should not be. With all my heart I wished that, when my neighbor glanced down at her watch she would have realized that the time of her children's childhood was getting away, and that rather than park the wagon she would have kept pulling it until her little girls waved themselves limp. Or at least just a little longer.

I speak to my children of these feelings I have. I tell them that what I do for them, things I used to think of as chores, I'm learning to think of as a temporary delight because I associate the tasks with the joy of having Rebecca and Bradley in my life.

For instance, when they were babies they loved to snack on dry Cheerios as they sat in the highchair. Because they hadn't mastered the hand-to-mouth routine, the kitchen floor became something akin to a minefield strewn with tiny, explosive *O*s. I'd clear the floor of all the *O*s I could find, but inevitably I missed some and would discover them only when I felt the irritating, explosive crunch beneath my shoes. Instead of having one *O* to pick up, I had a thousand specks to sweep.

Somewhere along life's timeline, however, after Bradley came along, I learned to react to these crunching explosions with a smile instead of a scowl. It had dawned on me that this was my moment in life for picking up Cheerios. When this moment was gone, my clumsy little boy would be gone. I would no longer have tiny Bradley to cuddle in my arms for as long as I pleased, to kiss until my pucker ran dry, and to rock in the evening hours with his tiny hand squeezing the tip of my finger and his velvet cheek resting flush against mine. Picking up Cheerio fragments, I had decided, was a good and glorious moment in my life.

I learned to transfer this new attitude to other chores eventually, though not to the chore of carrying kids during the summer we vacationed at Disney World, when Bradley was four and Rebecca was six. By any measure of distance, trudging through all of Disney's theme parks involves torturous amounts of walking. By the measure of stride for Bradley and Rebecca, about a third my size, the torture was tripled. So they climbed on me and their mom. I'm afraid I occasionally wore them like a painful, floating tumor that sometimes appeared atop my shoulders, or at other times midway up my back with tentacles clamped around my neck and waist, or at still other times on my gut, like a bloated belly I had to support with my arms. Only later did I realize that this was part of my carrying moment: that short time in life when child clings to parent and both grow weary together, wrapped in each other's arms.

Now, when a burst of unspoken resentment begins to spread over me as I drive Bradley to what seems like his five hundredth soccer practice, I look over at him sitting there with his short blond hair sticking up and his brilliant red shinguards popping out of the top of his high socks. I remind myself that this is my driving moment. Too soon he will be in his own car, driving away from me. But right now he's with me, and I love his being here. So I learn to love the drive.

I can't be sure that telling my kids about these feelings helps them cherish their childhood, but I know it helps me cherish it. I can hope that they will eventually see this in me and mimic the cherishing. After all, they mimic my foibles with distressing precision. It's only fair that they take the good with the bad.

CHAPTER 3

A Moment for School

Gold there is, and rubies in abundance,
but lips that speak knowledge are a rare jewel.
PROVERBS 20:15

I must have been only nine or ten years old, but the picture is sharp in my memory, perhaps because it was so startling. Still groggy from sleep, I had stumbled down the stairs on my way to breakfast to be followed by another winter's day at school. Our house was heated by an old coal-burning furnace converted to burn gas. The first person downstairs—usually Mom or me—turned the temperature up from the meat-locker setting Dad insisted on at night.

There was no forced air to propel heat into the house, just the slow and natural process of heat rising from the basement furnace. Sometimes we children would huddle together by the two living room heat registers at the base of the inside wall, to catch the first warm wafts of the morning. As the first child downstairs, I was generally guaranteed a prime location against the register directly above the furnace.

Not this morning. As I turned the corner from the staircase and walked through the doorway into the living room, I saw two figures already clustered there, sitting beneath the dim light of a single lamp. It was Mom and my little brother Cliff. They were looking at a book.

I asked what they were doing, and Mom simply said they were studying. Like this was perfectly normal for such a dark and frigid hour of the morning. It was remarkably abnormal for many reasons, not the least of which was that if we had held elections in my family, my blond, stubble-haired brother would have been voted most likely to succeed at sleeping. He was forever the last one out of bed. Sometimes I had to yank the covers down and let the cold air rush in upon him, forcing him to scramble and get dressed. Yet on this morning Mom had managed to get Cliff up without waking me, though he and I shared a room.

The house was already warming up, so I continued into the kitchen and fixed myself a bowl of cereal, thinking no more of the scene I had just glimpsed—a scene that would repeat itself morning after morning. In retrospect, the portrait of the two of them huddled together around a book is one of the most pitied yet heartwarming images from my childhood. You see, Cliff's school teachers had identified him as a slow learner. They held him back in kindergarten and again in first grade. He was devastated by this.

To my shame, I discovered that the most potent weapon I had to inflict injury on him was not my fists or my feet but my mouth. I would call him "Flunky" and remind him that he was the only kid I knew who had failed kindergarten.

When teachers told Mom that Cliff would never finish grade school, she became his tutor. The scene I had witnessed that cold Akron morning was the beginning of a long process that would eventually lead Cliff into a private school for several years, allow him to jump forward a grade, and culminate in his graduation from high school—celebrated at our house with the jubilation of VE Day, not Victory in Europe but Victory in Education.

School was critically important to my mom, perhaps because she had seen in her family and in her West Virginia hill-people neighbors the limitations of a life without it. Unfortunately, Mom had a hard time transferring her passion for education to her children. We hated school. All of us. I put up such a fuss throughout kindergarten that, when we moved to another neighborhood midway through the year, my folks decided not to enroll me in a new class. That made me a kindergarten dropout with no room to criticize my little brother. I cried the first day of school every year through third grade.

Aside from this temporary retreat, Mom insisted that all of her children go the full route to high school graduation—and beyond if we wanted. If any of us chose college, we would become the first on either side of our extended families to do so. Dad quit school in eighth grade to run the family farm while his dad and older brothers worked in the coal mines; Mom struggled through to graduation, hating every day of school and suffering wounds from teachers who said she'd never amount to anything.

The Biggest Regret of All

Now that I'm grown and looking back on this family history, one thing is incredibly clear: Mother knew best. Education is important.

This has been repeatedly confirmed by generations of social

psychologists who have been conducting studies to find out what people regret most in life. Throughout fifty years of research, in a gauntlet of studies from New York to California, one regret has consistently emerged as the chart-topping, biggest regret of all: not getting a better education.

It's bigger than regret about marrying the wrong person. Bigger than regret about not having kids. Bigger than regret about not spending more time with the family. Men, women, old, young, rich, poor, high school dropouts, college graduates—it doesn't matter. The most widespread regret among Americans is not taking their education more seriously, studying harder, or going longer. Even people with a master's degree regret not getting a doctorate, and Ph.D.'s regret not applying themselves more.

Rev. Billy Graham, who has preached to more people than any human who ever lived, and whose traveling crusade ministry has led some three million people to step forward and dedicate their lives to Jesus, had this to say for himself during a reflective interview with reporters: "I had one great failure, and that was intellectual."

He had studied at Bob Jones College, a strict Bible school in Tennessee where dates were chaperoned chats in the parlor and hand-holding was forbidden. He fled south to Florida Bible Institute, where he could play golf and date a pretty girl, who eventually broke off their relationship. But he later won a scholarship to Wheaton College in Illinois and finished his formal studies there, in one of the most respected undergraduate institutions of evangelical Christianity.

"I should have gone on," he lamented. "I do regret I didn't do enough reading, enough study, both formal and informal."

On the flip side of the same coin, people who have learned something, anything—a database of facts, a job, a hobby—tend never to regret the knowledge and skills they achieved. In a study at Cornell University in New York, as I mentioned earlier, no one said they regretted time spent developing a skill or a hobby, even if they had long since abandoned the activity.

This is true for me. I took flying lessons when I was in high school. Although I had a fear of heights—and still do when I look straight down a skyscraper wall or a mountain cliff—my uncle wanted a flying buddy, so he offered to pay for my training. I earned my pilot's license, but when I moved away from my hometown I discontinued the expensive hobby. Still, when I recall my flying days, it's with joy and a sense of accomplishment. I'll always feel grateful to my mom's big brother for allowing my self-esteem to soar during those teenage years, when my emerging sense of worth was so vulnerable and easily influenced for better or worse.

I'm even glad Mom talked me into taking accordion lessons. The accordion is the Rodney Dangerfield of instruments: it gets no respect. But I was raised in northeastern Ohio, national center for the polka arts and Polish sausage. I haven't touched either the accordion or Polish sausage in years, but I find satisfaction in recalling that I once had the strength to lug around an instrument that weighed nearly as much as I did, the discipline to practice each day, and the fortitude to overcome stage fright and actually play the accordion a few times in church.

I particularly enjoy remembering the look on my pastor's face after I opened my music book to "The Beer Barrel Polka." On the facing page, which he apparently couldn't see, was "Whispering Hope," the song I played. That memory alone is worth all the accordion lessons.

A Moment for College

When I became the first person in the known history of my mountain-bred family to enroll in college, my mother came along. Not to be available in case I burst into tears but to start working on a degree of her own—to become a school teacher.

With five kids, one graduated and four others in high school and junior high, she already knew a thing or two about teaching and about the public school system. But she was terrified about becoming a student again, twenty years after high school. She said that, out of all the people close to her, I was the only one who encouraged her to go back to school.

Apparently, Dad couldn't get excited about exchanging a full-time housewife for a part-time wife, part-time student. Others in the family thought the idea was dumb and dumber, and that for even the feistiest, most energetic of redheads, trying to juggle a college schedule and a large family was like trying to juggle Dumbo and his mother. I have no memory of saying anything that would have led Mom to believe she could do what could be done only in cartoons. But she says I told her that, if she wanted to do it, she should. So she did it. And she got better grades than I did.

As it turns out, her decision was a wise one. She launched herself into a fulfilling career. And she contributed immeasurable financial stability to the family; about five years after Dad argued that his job provided adequately for the family, he was diagnosed with cancer and began a long and expensive treatment regime that would eventually force him into early retirement.

Knowing what this teaching degree meant to Mom and my family is the main reason I later encouraged my wife to get back into nursing school. Linda had dropped out before we met and was working as a nurse's aide. But I believed that completing her degree would assure her of a career she enjoyed, and it would give our family the best insurance policy I could imagine. In fact, the stability of Linda's job is the reason I was later able to risk starting a freelance writing business that allowed me to work out of a home office.

Helping Our Kids Become Good Students

As Rebecca's fifth summer drew swiftly to a close, and kindergarten loomed ahead, I became afraid for her. Would she scream in terror when Linda and I walked from the classroom and left her with a bunch of strangers, as I had done as a youngster? Would she have teachers who were repelled by children, as I occasionally had—uncouth educators who slapped faces, pulled hair, and spanked the entire class for the infraction of one student? Would she wake up each morning dreading the school day ahead?

What took place on Rebecca's last day of kindergarten pretty well sums up how that first year went. As the tiny students began lining up to leave the school, Rebecca walked over to her teacher, hugged her, kissed her, and said, "Thank you for being my teacher." Rebecca said her teacher replied, "Thank you for being in my class." And with that, the lady silently cried. "I saw a tear fall down," Rebecca told me.

Just a few days earlier I had written her teacher, Elaine Broockerd, this letter. I sent copies to the principal and to the superintendent of schools.

Dear Mrs. Broockerd:

Before the school year ends I'd like to tell you how fortunate Linda and I feel to have had you as Rebecca's very first public school teacher.

You got her formal education off to a great start.

Frankly, I was worried about that. I didn't start liking school until college. In fact, I cried the first day of school through third grade. It became an annual ritual. So you can understand why I was concerned that Rebecca get off to an enjoyable start.

You helped her do just that. She has developed a genuine love for both you and school. Thank you for earning her love.

And thanks for sending her to the principal's office so often. I remember going to see the principal only once in my life. Coincidentally, it was when I was in kindergarten. The teacher sent me there because I wouldn't stop crying for my mom. How much better my memory could have been had the teacher sent me there with a redeemable coupon for a hug and a kiss from the principal. [This was a reward system that the principal used, assisted by Hershey's Kisses.]

Linda has had several opportunities to work with you in class and to express to you her appreciation for the job you are doing. But I haven't. You and Geri Grady [the principal] and the office staff all have my deepest appreciation for the loving concern you have shown to the most precious little girl in my life.

In a couple of years I'll be sending your way the most precious little boy in my life.

Encore.

The principal got her copy of the letter first. Rebecca's teacher said Mrs. Grady came rushing down the hall, waving the letter like a flag and asking, "Did you get your letter yet?" "What letter?" Rebecca's teacher replied. "You better go to your mailbox," the principal answered. "I'm taking Mr. Sunderland his copy now." He was the superintendent, who worked in the same building complex. Judging by this exuberance, educators don't get nearly enough praise.

Bradley drew the same kindergarten teacher, and he, too, enjoyed a wonderful first year. And second. And third. And on and on. Both children love school and are performing well, and my wife and I are intent on doing whatever we can to make sure our kids get the most out of this moment in their lives.

So when an editor offered me the assignment of interviewing educators around the country, to find out how parents can help their children become better students, I snatched it. Here are a few highlights of what I learned. Some of the advice applies not only to kids but to anyone serious about their studies.

School Begins at Home

Children who are not mentally challenged before kindergarten are never going to be what they could have been, according to many educators. For some types of development, there is an early and narrow window of opportunity for wiring the child's brain.

A baby whose eyes are clouded by cataracts from birth may have those cataracts removed at age two. But by then it's too late; the blindness is permanent. A similar principle applies to learning. Preschoolers exposed to music or foreign languages develop a neural wiring system more extensive and more powerful than those of other children.

Kids who learn two languages at the same time will speak both of them like natives, while those of us who begin our studies in high school will usually remain plagued with a strong accent. Japanese adults learning English, for instance, find it difficult and often impossible to distinguish between the sounds of "ra" and "la" because, in the Japanese language, the sound of *r*'s and *l*'s are merged. So "hello" becomes "helrow."

Early on, my wife and I discovered that Rebecca loved music: listening to it, dancing to it, and singing along. So we've showered her with CD's, cassette tapes, radios, a boom box, and a karaoke system. If you can name a hit song currently playing on the radio, she'll likely know the lyrics to it. She's developing a beautiful singing voice and learning to accompany herself on the piano.

Her brother, on the other hand, loves sports more than music (though for some mysterious reason he seems to enjoy the blues and has just started playing the saxophone in the school band). He relishes living in the seasonal cycle of spring and autumn soccer, summer baseball, and winter basketball. Lately he's been threatening to add football, the crunching game that injures more American children each year than any other organized sport. But that's another chapter: "A Moment for the ER."

Feed Them Breakfast

Hungry kids don't have the energy to be good students. Portland area health teacher and registered nurse Ginny Markell, a former chair of the health and welfare commission for the National Parent Teacher Association and now the PTA's president-elect, expresses it vividly.

She says that every day she sees what happens when kids skip breakfast: "They float through their first two periods of the day and collapse on us at ten o'clock in the morning." They may retain consciousness, but little else.

Get Them to Bed at a Decent Hour

"I think elementary school children should be in bed by 8:30," Markell says. Young children, she explains, are experiencing a period of intense physical and emotional growth, which takes a lot of energy.

"Kids who are well rested perform better in school," says Brenda Nixon, mother of two and a full-time parent educator. "They're more mentally alert."

Physicians who specialize in sleep disorders say that sleep requirements among children vary, just as they do among adults. But on the average, kids ages five to nine need about eleven to twelve hours of sleep, kids ages ten to fourteen need eight to ten hours, and older teens need eight to nine.

For kids of any age, early to bed can mean early to rise, allowing slow starters the extra time they need to acclimate to the vertical dimension. Some kids need fifteen minutes to fasten the Velcro straps on their shoes, says Markell. "If that's what they need, then that's what we should allow for," she says. "If we're the adult constantly yelling at them to hurry up, I think it chips away at their self-esteem." A poor self-image carries over into school by programming the kids to think they can't do anything right.

In our house, at the moment, we have a name for 8 P.M. on school nights. We call it "Feet off the Floor." By then, the kids are to be done with their nightly routine and lying in bed reading, listening to music, or simply relaxing as they unwind from the day. Thirty minutes later is "Lights Out," unless they need a little extra time to finish a chapter.

Clue In the Teacher to Problems at Home

"I don't need nitty-gritty details," says elementary teacher Marilyn Mokhtarian of Olathe, Kansas. "But I do have parents who tell me if there are rough times between the husband and wife. And I appreciate it, because that's a major factor that affects children."

Without this peek into the family life, all the teacher sees is a disruptive child. So the teacher might respond with punishment, instead of reassurance that could quickly calm the child and help him get on with the business of studying.

"I had a mother the other day scribble me a note," Mokhtarian said. "She wrote, 'We just had a really bad morning. Watch out for Sam'[the name has been changed]. Their alarm hadn't gone off, and his sister threw a temper tantrum. As Sam was handing me the note he was bouncing off the walls, rushing around, yelling. If I hadn't known what he had come from, I'd have been saying, 'Sam, sit down! Sam, stop the talking!' Instead I could say, 'Hey, Sam. Man, it was kinda wild at home.' He rolled his eyes and said, 'Yeah, that's right.' And I said, 'But you know it's OK here. Mom and sister will feel better when you get home.' I was able to reassure him and get him calmed down and in control of himself. The day went reasonably well for him.

"The kids are with me for seven to eight hours a day," Mokhtarian says. "If they're feeling frightened or sad, I need to know that. How are they going to learn if their whole mind is filled up with, 'Oh my goodness, Grandma's in the hospital'? If I don't know what's going on, I can't help them."

High school teacher Dee Richardson of an Oklahoma City suburb says she doesn't often get notes from parents, but she does get phone calls. "Sometimes they'll just call the counselor, and the counselor will send a note to the teachers."

Get Involved in School
Go to parent-teacher conferences. Join your child's class on a field trip. Volunteer to teach something you know. Call, just to see how your child's doing. Parents who do these things end up with kids who achieve more in school.

Unfortunately, parents often avoid school because they think they'd only get in the way. Teachers admit that they used to think of parents as more of an intrusion than a help. But no more. Educators have been embracing the old proverb "It takes a village to raise a child."

The U.S. Department of Education recently confirmed what other studies in California and Iowa earlier revealed—and what my mom discovered many years ago, after spending weeks of early morning hours tutoring her son: students do better in school when their parents get involved. Researchers for the Department of Education interviewed parents and guardians of seventeen thousand students in kindergarten through twelfth grade and found that, when both parents were involved at school, 50 percent of the students got mostly *A*'s on their report cards. But when parents got involved no more than once a year, only 27 percent of the students got mostly A's.

Don't Criticize the Teacher in Front of Your Kids
"We have it all the time, parents telling their kids that the teachers are dumb," says Kristina Elias, principal of a middle school in Hebron, Connecticut. "You report that to the parent and the parent says, 'Well, I guess I said something like that.' Well, how do you expect us to teach any regard for school or academics if this is what you're saying to your kid?"

Bill McBride, a Colorado State University English professor who educates future teachers, advises parents to calmly discuss the situation with the child before flying off the handle and making rash judgments. If the situation warrants it, speak directly with the teacher.

Linda and I have occasionally needed to talk with teachers of both our children about problems that cropped up. Once Bradley was put on in-school suspension for something he didn't do. This meant he was given a stack of schoolwork to do while sitting in the corner of another teacher's room. After school, when I heard Bradley's account of what had happened, I became silently furious. I, too, had been unfairly punished in school.

The next morning I arranged a phone conference with his teacher. I actually managed to stay calm, though the tension was thick when our conversation began. Once the teacher investigated the matter further, she decided that she owed Bradley an apology. I also asked the teacher not to discipline Bradley in this manner without first contacting Linda or me, so we could talk with him while the incident was still fresh.

Don't Try to Block School Discipline

"Just today a student got a detention," said principal Kristina Elias, "but after school he wanted to go to a baseball game with the other kids. The parent called and said the boy was needed after school to mind his baby brother. We said the boy told us he wanted to go to the game. And the parent said, 'Oh well, yeah, he called me and asked if I would call you and get him out of detention because he could do it any time.' You want to say, 'Just let the kid be responsible for his own wrong behavior. Please don't get involved here.' But you say, 'Let's play together on this.'"

When parents and teachers do play together, Elias said, and it dawns on the kids that they'll be held accountable for their actions at school, they start taking their education more seriously. They also learn valuable lessons not written into the curriculum.

Michael Calvert, a Los Angeles area bank manager and father of five, watched this happen. The school called and said his fifth-grade son was caught in a group of eight kids taunting a special education student during recess. Calvert met with the principal and talked about how to discipline the boy in a way that would teach him a thing or two.

"We came up with a plan that my son should spend his recess time working with the special education teachers and with the entire class of kids," Calvert says, "just so he understands what they have to face on a day-to-day basis and can get a clear understanding of how harmful his behavior was."

The boy did this for a month. He helped the class start a basketball team and taught them some of the skills needed to play the game. "He really liked it," his father says. "And he learned a lot."

Calvert says he takes seriously any reports of his children misbehaving in school, even if the offense seems out of character for the child. "We do know our children better than the teacher does," he says. "But on the other hand they know them better in the school environment than we do."

Talk to Them About What They're Doing in School

"I know it's hard," says elementary teacher Marilyn Mokhtarian. "You ask them what they did in school today and they'll say, 'Oh, nothing.'

"You have to ask specific questions. 'What book did you read today?' 'What are you working on in math?' This takes a minute or two," Mokhtarian says, "and I know that parents have hectic schedules. But I also know that the kids who seem to retain the most have parents who do this."

When parents find out what the kids are studying, they tend to pitch in and help with what Mokhtarian calls "teachable one-minute moments." Dad finds out his first grader is learning to count coins, so he invites the child to count the change in his pocket. This shows that Dad is interested in school, and it rubs off on the child.

Asking your kids about their day also makes them feel important. "If children come into my classroom feeling good about themselves," Mokhtarian says, "I can teach them a lot easier. They want to participate, raise their hands, offer opinions, take chances. They want to learn because Mom and Dad have said, 'Wow, you're adding and subtracting double digits? Man alive, you must be smart!' Well, yeah, they think they are smart then. And they want to learn more."

Talk About What's Bothering Them

"A situation that seems minor to a parent may have great significance to a child," says Willie Mae Crews, English program specialist for Birmingham, Alabama schools. Maybe someone teased or threatened your youngster. Maybe your child is the tallest in the class, or the heaviest, or the only one with red hair. Maybe the body sculpting caused by puberty has left your teenager perplexed and embarrassed about the changes—or lack of changes.

"The child can become so obsessed with being different that he will not spend time learning," Crews says. "At times like this the parent can say, 'You know, it's all right to be taller than another child. If we look around us in life there are short people, average height people, tall people.'"

Many kids are missing not only *this* kind of dialogue with their mom and dad but *any* substantial dialogue. In a recent study among eighth graders, one in five said they had not had a ten-minute conversation with either parent in the past month.

Insist That They Do Their Homework

"There's all kind of research that says that 98 percent of kids who do homework succeed in school," says principal Kristina Elias. "Homework reinforces what they just learned. It's like vocabulary: if you use a word three times it's yours. It's the same thing with homework. It's not going to be a take on one shot."

In our house, homework gets done before the kids leave the premises to play. We don't insist that they start their homework the minute they arrive. They need to unwind just as Linda and I do after a hard day's work. But before supper, or sometimes after, the homework gets done.

Let Your Children See You Reading

"Kids need to see that reading's important in the home," says high school teacher Dee Richardson. "It's real easy for them to see that reading is something you *have* to do—it's an assignment, it's to satisfy a teacher. But if you're going to get young people to be lifelong readers so they can become lifelong learners, they need to see that reading is enjoyable."

Some evenings in our home, Linda and I will each grab a magazine or a book and join our kids in the thirty-minute "Feet off the Floor" reading time. We even sit in bed beside them.

Limit the TV Viewing

"Everything we see in PTA says that children should not be looking at more than two hours of television a day," says Markell. "But some kids have seen that even before Mom or Dad get home from work." On average, kids watch three to four hours of TV a day, according to Nielsen Media Research. That's roughly a twenty-four-hour day every week, a seventh of their lives as children.

The problem with most TV viewing is that it doesn't require a flexing muscle or a snapping synapse. It can turn a kid fat and dumb. "We've seen a great weight increase in this particular generation of kids," Markell says. "The more they sit and watch, the more they eat." And the less they do other things—like read a book, play outside, or find their niche in extracurricular activities at school.

Ten years ago, a fourth of children ages three to seventeen were overweight, reports Princeton Survey Research Associates, Inc. Now almost a third are too plump. Memphis researcher Robert Klesges said that part of the reason is that a child's metabolic rate drops while sitting in a trancelike state in front of the TV. To make matters worse, a kid in that trance does not see a lot of messages about broccoli. An hour of children's TV dishes up twenty-one commercials, a San Diego study reports. About half of them are selling something to eat; more than 90 percent of that food is high in fat, sugar, or salt.

Not all TV, however, will fatten your kids and fry their brains. Educational TV, such as "Sesame Street," improved the verbal and math scores of elementary age children, according to a study done by the Center for Research on the Influences of Television on Children at the University of Kansas.

Point Them Toward Extracurricular Activities, But Don't Push

"If you can get them involved in something at school they're interested in, the success rate is remarkable," says high school teacher Dee Richardson.

Richardson explains that the reason grades go up among students who take part in cocurricular activities like working on the yearbook, serving on the student council, or even running a football into a wall of muscle and bone is that once they get a taste of success, they want more. "They say, 'If I can do this, then I can probably do something else.'"

It also generates school pride, a motivation booster of the same voltage that prods employees of respected firms to work harder. And if school pride isn't enough to produce better grades, eligibility rules certainly add a few joules to the voltage.

You can overdo it, though.

"Some kids are under enormous pressure to please their parents in terms of taking every top course, and doing cheerleading, sports, drama," says middle school principal Kristina Elias. "They're ready to drop. They're exhausted."

Keep Work Hours Reasonable

"That's probably the biggest problem I have in my classroom: students working and trying to keep up with school," says high school teacher Dee Richardson.

"I've got students who work forty hours a week in addition to going to school. They go to work at four o'clock in the afternoon and they get off at midnight. When do they possibly have time for schoolwork?"

This problem isn't isolated to just a few students, Richardson says. More than 100 of her 140 students work at least part-time. Nationwide, three out of four high school juniors and seniors hold down jobs. Richardson said that nearly half of her students work so much that it hurts them academically. "They don't get enough sleep, so when they get to school that's all they want to do."

Eight to ten hours a week is the ideal job for a teenager, says Bryna Shore Fraser, deputy director of the National Institute for Work and Learning, a research group in Washington, D.C. Teenagers, she said, should work no more than the equivalent of one evening a week and one weekend afternoon. This leaves them time for homework, extracurricular activities, and sleep.

Don't Overemphasize Grades

"I am disturbed about basing the full assessment of the child on grades alone," says Willie Mae Crews. "Grades will tell you only what the child knows about what the child was tested on."

Parents shouldn't demand all *A*'s, adds principal Kristina

Elias. "When you do, kids start cheating. They start finding ways to get *A*'s." Another popular *A*-maker strategy is to pick the easiest teachers and classes.

What Michael Calvert asks of his five kids is not for row upon row of As—or Bs, for that matter. He asks that they do the best they can. Some of his children are always on the honor roll. One, however, is never there and probably never will be. The child is a gifted athlete, though.

"He expects the NBA will draft him right out of junior high school," Calvert said. "I'm sure it's hard for him when we're constantly going to award night for this one and picking up a scholarship award for that one. He's never going to be in that group. But we tell him, 'You may not make it to the honor roll, but you have to make sure you're doing the very best you can and that you're completing the work and doing exactly what the instructors are telling you. If you're not, you're the person who's going to lose out.'"

Hug Them When They Feel Defeated

Perhaps your child failed an important test, didn't get the lead in the school play, or got cut from the first-string team.

"A well-timed hug," says Willie Mae Crews, "helps children see that failure is only temporary." Just because they didn't do well this time is no indication they will never, ever do well. "What you want to do," she says, "is encourage your child that it's perseverance that produces success."

The apostle Paul said it another way, putting a positive spin on the rough times: "Suffering produces perseverance; perseverance, character; and character, hope. And hope does not disappoint us" (Romans 5:3-5). Yet I have a feeling Paul would have agreed that a hug helps too.

The school years can be trying, troubling years. But they're worth the trouble, for out of knowledge flows wisdom and out of wisdom flows the power to live one moment at a time. For this reason, "Wise men store up knowledge" (Proverbs 10:14).

CHAPTER 4

A Moment
With a Friend

Jonathan became one in spirit with David,
and he loved him as himself.
1 SAMUEL 18:1

Having a close friend is not always an uplifting experience. A friend can suck the life force right out of you.

Consider two best friends I know, sixth-grade girls. I'm going to let you read a letter that one girl wrote to the other, but I'm going to change their names since I want to live.

Here's the background. The letter writer, whom I'll sardonically call Frieda Hollar, has invited her girlfriend Anna to attend a sleep-over birthday party with about half a dozen other preteen girls. Anna, however, has already accepted a previous invitation to the sleep-over of another friend, Gloria Hummel. Anna has never spent the night at Gloria's home, has been looking forward to the party for weeks, and has resisted pressure from both Frieda and Frieda's mother to bow out of the other party. Frieda has even reminded Anna that it's Frieda's mom, not Gloria's, who often drives both girls to school so they won't have to ride the overcrowded school bus. To no avail.

Resigned to Anna's decision, or maybe in a last desperate

attempt at persuasion, Frieda writes the following letter. I haven't corrected any misspellings or the bizarre punctuation because this letter is a masterpiece of authenticity and emotion. And I'm not touching it.

Dear Anna,

You and I's friendship is over! Your not invited to my birthday party! By the way I wasn't trying to break you and Gloria Hummel up. I don't know what I did to you for me to deserve this! You don't know how much you hurt me! I wasn't trying to do anything to hurt you! You and I weren't meant to be friends. You need to start to get your own ride to school, even if that means you riding the bus! Gloria Hummel is nice, but she considers me as a snob! She's not one of my best friends, she's not really even my friend, but sometimes I wish she were! I'm sorry! (but I think you need to start to respect me for who I am!) I'm really not trying to be rude! But if you think I am I'm not! I'm just trying to make a point! I don't like the way you are treating me! I know you don't know what I'm talking about but if you do, you know where I'm coming from! Please don't takes this badley!! I'm sorry but it's not going to work out! Good Bye!

Your ex-best friend,
Frieda Hollar.

P.S. Please, we may not make up, but until we do, you will not hear from me and please don't call!

Though the postscript seems to strip away all possibility of restoring the friendship, Anna is a smart little cookie who wasn't about to lose her friend, let alone her ride to school with winter approaching. The two worked out a compromise. Anna spent the early evening feasting and frolicking with Frieda and friends, then Anna's mom shuttled her to Gloria's bash. Happy ending. And happy birthday, Frieda.

Friends in Deed

Our friends, both inside and outside our family, are the most important people we know. They share our good times and bad, laughing with us and sometimes crying for us even when we don't realize it.

The parents of one of my son's buddies recently separated and started talking about divorce. The wife left her husband and three children. To pick up the financial slack, the father took a second job. He's not home a lot these days. His two girls are in high school and can take care of many of their basic needs without Dad. But the young boy, whom I'll call Billy, is only in fourth grade, so he spends a lot of time at the home of his grandparents, who fortunately live only a few miles away. Bradley and Billy play on a sports team together, so I've gotten to know Billy's grandpa as we stand on the sidelines and watch the practice. He said that, since the separation, his grandson has become afraid to be alone. Though Billy has his own bedroom at his grandparent's home, he won't sleep there. He prefers his grandparents' bedroom and took to sleeping on the floor beside their bed. The problem became so persistent that his grandpa bought the boy a cot.

Recently, while Billy spent a Saturday night with us, he told Bradley about this fear of being alone. A few nights later, shortly after Bradley went to bed, he began crying—gently at first, then in heaving sobs. I rushed into his room, but Linda had gotten there first and was already trying to comfort him. I couldn't imagine what would make a fifth-grade boy weep with such intensity.

"When I close my eyes," Bradley said, "I keep seeing Billy all alone and afraid."

No words that Linda or I spoke could calm our son. Though it was a school night, I carried him out to the living room and let him lie on the couch and fall asleep when he was good and ready, while I read nearby.

I've heard plenty of great definitions of friendship, but none more moving than the sound of one little boy crying on behalf of another. A strong contender, though, is a sentence fragment from my daughter. When Rebecca was ten years old and we got news that my dad's cancer had returned and infiltrated his left temple and bone marrow, I tried to prepare our children for what they might experience during our visit to my childhood home. "When we go to Ohio," I said, "one thing you'll notice is that our relatives will be crying. If you see them crying ..."

Rebecca interrupted me and finished the sentence. "I'll join with them," she said. And when the time came, she did. Fortunately, radiation destroyed the cancer in Dad's temple, resolving the immediate crisis.

Rebecca was a friend to her hurting family. Bradley was a friend to his teammate. Anna managed to remain friends with the birthday girl. Who are our friends?

"A friend is someone who walks in when everyone else

walks out," wrote Walter Winchell, a radio broadcaster and newspaper columnist in the early 1900s. Mary Schmich, a columnist for the *Chicago Tribune*, wrote much the same by distinguishing between "little *f* friends" and "big *F* friends." "When you get a disease or a divorce, a little *f* friend drops out of sight because she doesn't know what to say. A big *F* friend finds something to say."

Jesus described the ultimate "big *F* friend." As he struggled to explain the approaching crucifixion to his distressed disciples, Jesus said, "Greater love has no one than this, that he lay down his life for his friends" (John 15:13). Although we all needed the sacrificial death of Jesus, most of us will never need a friend to die for us. But we can certainly count on needing what the sages of Proverbs described: a friend who "sticks closer than a brother" (18:24) and who "loves at all times ... born for adversity" (17:17)—the person who comes near when everyone else walks away.

My family faced adversity one miserable weekend in January when we all came down with the flu. Linda got sick first and worst, winding up admitted to the hospital after smoking a thermometer to 104 degrees and melting her face into Neapolitan bags of pale white and flush pink. Her last words to me as I left the hospital were to bring her a change of clothes the next day. I didn't see her for three days.

By evening, two-year-old Rebecca and four-month-old Bradley were barking croupy coughs and I was beginning to feel an unexplainable jet-lag sensation. In the wee hours of the morning the virus hit hard enough to wake me. My head pulsated and my entire body ached as though I'd been run over by a stampede of Clydesdales. I remember lying motionless in bed and thinking that aspirin would help, but I was too weak to get up and walk the four steps to the medicine cabinet. So I settled for a night of drifting in and out of sleep, constantly checking the clock. Each time I awakened I was surprised to find that so little time had passed, and I was thankful that it was the aching that woke me instead of Bradley crying for a bottle or a dry diaper.

Bradley normally woke once or twice a night, but not that night. He normally rose at 6 A.M., but not that morning. By about 7 A.M., during my ache-induced jolts to consciousness, the thought began crossing my mind that the kids may have died in their sleep. Yet I didn't move.

In retrospect, it's hard for me to understand why I didn't drag myself out of bed and check on them. After all, I was the concerned dad who had worried so much about baby Rebecca's nighttime feedings, two years earlier, that on the first night she "overslept" her midnight meal, I awakened her—against the wishes of her mother, who is a pediatric nurse. I apparently felt that a father's intuition takes precedence over a four-year degree in nursing and several years of hospital nursing experience.

Bradley eventually woke with a whine at 8:30, which in turn woke Rebecca, who began coughing with a wet gurgle and speaking with the low baritone of a truck driver who had trouble pronouncing his r's. Out came the thermometers. Rebecca's temp was 100.7, Bradley's was 100.9, and mine was 101. I called my wife, who said she had slept well and was feeling much better, thank you. She advised me to pack up the kids and take them to our family doctor.

The earliest open slot in the doctor's appointment schedule was 2:05 that afternoon. We arrived on time and waited until three o'clock, though there was no one else in the waiting room. Perhaps it was the fever, but I began to imagine our doctor holed up in one of his three examination rooms, doing an outpatient liver transplant.

Rebecca found enough energy to wander to the magazine stack, pick up a medical journal, rip out a page, crumple it up, and bring the wad to me. What a profound comment on our situation, I remember thinking. I wanted to rip out a page myself, but the receptionist was watching. So I told Rebecca, "That's not an acceptable thing to do."

Our doctor intended to keep Linda in the hospital until Tuesday, but after seeing us he decided to keep her in until Wednesday. He thought if he released her on time, she'd come home, start taking care of us, and have a relapse. The doctor said we had a virus and antibiotics wouldn't help. So he told us to take pain relievers, decongestant, and cough medicine, drink fluids until our gums wrinkled, and get plenty of rest. By the time we got home at 3:30, we had the capacity to do only the last of the above. With both of my arms heaped full of children, I climbed the thirteen stairs from the garage to the living room. There, we all collapsed onto the couch. I should have given everyone a round of medicine, but clinging together as three in one, we began to dematerialize into the cushions.

Bradley sat spineless on my lap. Eyes swollen, cheeks and eyebrows a hot poker red, face drooping into the expression-less sag of complete exhaustion, and head limp upon my left shoulder. He looked as if he had just finished four weeks of hard labor on the railroad. Rebecca sat at my right side, her saucer face turned forward and her full moon eyes staring out of focus and blinking a slow drum. We fell asleep right there, sitting up.

I have had many friends in my life but none whom I

cherish more than the ones who came knocking at my door to help me with what must have seemed to them no more than small acts of kindness. Yet they did nothing less than trans-figure misery into glorious comfort. We were hungry, and they fed us. We were weary, and they gave us rest.

The strain of flu that struck my family drained nearly every ounce of energy from us yet left our appetites intact. At supper time, two friends from my Sunday school class brought us a hot meal. I still remember it, delicious and warm: home-made chicken pot pie and a bowl of scrumptious noodles. For dessert, gourmet ice cream blended with cookies and cream. Flu hell had become flu heaven.

Another friend from my Sunday school class, a nurse and a woman of propriety beyond question, offered to stay with us that night and watch the kids so I could get some uninter-rupted sleep. I'm sorry to say I declined the offer, explaining that I didn't want her to infect her family with the bug.

In fact, I was afraid of what others would think of her spending the night while my wife was gone. How un-Christlike of me, I now believe. Jesus allowed himself to be fed by tax collectors, Jews who were detested as traitors collabo-rating with the occupying Roman forces. And he permitted a woman with a bad reputation to publicly express her loving gratitude by kissing his feet and anointing him with expensive, fragrant oil. Yet I turned away a sincere and godly woman whose help I needed.

Fortunately, she didn't give up. A few days later, when Rebecca required a return visit to the doctor, the woman came to baby-sit Bradley. During that time, she vacuumed our house, cleaned our bathrooms, and prepared homemade soup from fixings she brought.

I don't know that these friends saw my family's plight as an embraceable, fleeting moment in time—a tiny window of opportunity to show themselves friends with a capital *F*. But that's exactly what it was. Not before nor since have they had another chance to befriend my family in such a meaningful and memorable way.

All of these friends have long since moved away, but I will never forget what they did for my family. Whenever someone mentions one of their names or I smell chicken pot pie baking in the oven or homemade soup simmering on the stove, their faces come to mind and my spirit smiles.

Reaching for Friendship

Some people are socially gifted. They make friends easily. Others, like me, are socially challenged and better suited to bonding with the cast of a television series. I'm partial to the original crew of the starship *Enterprise;* may they live long and prosper.

I wish I could make friends as easily as Linda and the kids do. The first time I remember wishing this was on a hot summer day a couple of months before Rebecca began first grade. I took her to the school playground, to familiarize her with what would soon become her new stomping ground.

Playing on the swing set was another little girl about Rebecca's age, with her dad watching nearby. The instant Rebecca got within speaking distance of the girl, Rebecca asked, "Wanna play?" That's all it took. They chattered and played together until the other girl had to leave. The father and I never even made eye contact. But I chuckled at the thought of how he might respond if I walked over to him and asked, "Wanna play?"

As odd as that childlike question sounds, we adults often use only a disguised, more stately version of it when we try launching a friendship. We invite someone over for dinner, or to a movie, or to a Christmas bell concert at church. At least that's what we do if we're brave enough to risk being turned down.

I'm not particularly brave, so most of the friends I've had are the ones who did the asking. On those rare occasions when I did ask, I tended to make offers that no person this side of dementia would refuse. Such as, "My wife and I would like to cut your grass for free this summer." I said that to a neighbor, not really to make friends as much as to help preserve his marriage. He's a workaholic who was recovering from a heart attack and, by doctor's orders, was to stay away from his lawnmower. When he disobeyed—and he was a repeat offender—his wife lit up like a highway flare alongside a wreck.

This was a window of opportunity for my wife and me to befriend our neighbor. He accepted our offer and a week later gave me the key to his backyard gate. When he handed me the key, I thought it was to give me convenient access to the largest section of his lawn, but he said it was so our kids could use his pool whenever they wanted. The key pulled double duty that summer. Afterward, our neighbor told us to keep it for hot times ahead. We still have it and use it.

Whether we reach for friendship the brave way or my way, there's something spiritual that takes place in the reaching. Ironically, it took a monk in a Trappist monastery, an isolated man in a secluded place of worship, to help me discover this truth about friendship. Father Jeff Behrens, writing from a

Georgia monastery for the *National Catholic Reporter*, said that when it comes to friendship, "the reaching is more real than the finding." I read that and said, "Huh?"

But as I thought about his perplexing statement, I found in the cobwebs of my memory a theology lesson from my seminary days. A professor had told our class that many ancient Greek philosophers, including Plato, believed that this world is just a deceptive shadow of the spiritual world. The philosophers compared living in this world to living in a cave, explaining that we see only what amounts to shadows cast on the cave wall from the real objects outside the cave. Since in this physical world we are confined to what amounts to little more than a cave, the philosophers taught, the shadows look real to us—but they're only dark, distorted outlines of objects projecting them.

The writer of Hebrews seemed to pick up on this idea by explaining that the law of Moses, which for more than a millennium had pointed Jews toward holiness, "is only a shadow of the good things that are coming—not the realities themselves" (Hebrews 10:1).

Perhaps reaching for friendship is a spiritual act of love, and the friendship it produces is just a shadow of the good and everlasting experience awaiting us beyond the cave and in the kingdom. If so, the reaching out in love—bravely or otherwise—is a celestial behavior that we can and should begin practicing now.

Jesus reached out for friends at the very time many of us tend to withdraw: when life got tough. A few hours before the arrest that would lead to his execution, he called together his twelve closest friends for a last meal and he asked to be remembered. While waiting for the arresting officers, he pulled aside his three most intimate friends and implored them to pray with him. Then, while dying on the cross, he asked the Father, the Supreme Friend, not to abandon him. Jesus knew the value of friends.

Studies conducted by health-care researchers from Finland to California confirm that friends are, indeed, of great value. Friends help us in many ways. They become a sounding board, insightful consultants who know us well enough to help us solve our problems. They give material help: money, muscle, the shirts off their backs. They offer emotional support that lifts our self-image and reduces the physically damaging effects of stress.

For example, research has shown that people with a strong support group recover more quickly from illness and surgery, have a higher immune response to disease, and even have lower cholesterol levels. If a friend can make us laugh, all the better, for a hundred laughs is the aerobic equivalent of ten minutes spent rowing, according to a study done at Stanford University School of Medicine. Obviously social creatures, we human beings actually live longer when we have friends, and we die at a comparatively young age if we isolate ourselves.

Friendship has always been important, but it's even more so in today's mobile culture, in which people fling themselves far from home and depend on friends for the kind of support they used to get from their family. I live eight hundred miles from my parents, brothers, and sisters. When my car breaks down, they can't usually help. (Once, however, I carried the phone to the garage and had my dad listen to me try to start the car. He correctly diagnosed a busted starter, then walked me through the steps to replace it. I vividly recall my trepidation as I turned the key after installing the new starter. But the engine cranked up without pause, and I was instantly swept into spiritual exhilaration, thanking both Jesus and my dad. You'd understand if you ever saw me with a wrench.)

As important as true friends are, they are all too rare.

"You have very few friends in life," said Chicago Mayor Richard M. Daley, commenting on one of the many scandals that plagued his administration. "And those who say they're your friends—many of them are not your friends."

Like politics, the movie industry is also famous for decimating friendships. Film producer Jean Doumanian, who has produced *Saturday Night Live* and films such as *Mighty Aphrodite* and *Bullets Over Broadway,* said her father once gave her this warning: "You're lucky if you have the same number of friends in life as you have fingers on one hand."

In fact, when Jesus came to the end of his life, he had only four friends standing near him as he hung on the cross: his mother, an aunt, Mary Magdalene, and an unnamed disciple presumed to have been John (see John 19:25-26). To paraphrase Walter Winchell, these were the people who walked into Jesus' life when everyone else walked out.

When the moment comes that we find such friends as these—or can become such a friend to another—we should snatch up the chance. Otherwise, the moment will come and the moment will go. What will remain is a friend or nothing at all.

In those fleeting instants when we find ourselves among friends, we should savor the time. We are blown here and there by the winds of culture, not knowing who will be gone tomorrow on a whirlwind quest for a new job, a new church, or a change of scenery. Even those who remain nearby will not stay as long as we would like. For, as the psalmist sang to God,

"You have made my days a mere handbreadth; the span of my years is as nothing before you. Each man's life is but a breath" (Psalm 39:5). God gives that breath, and in his time he takes it away.

When cherished friends have gone, we will believe that they have gone too soon. In this moment of the meantime, let us bask in the pleasure of their company, living our friendships to the fullest. When disputes occasionally erupt, producing messages that scream, "You and I's friendship is over!" we take a lesson from a sixth grader and untangle the mess. Friends are worth the trouble.

CHAPTER 5

A Moment
for Your Love

Jacob served seven years to get Rachel,
but they seemed like only a few days to him
because of his love for her.
GENESIS 29:20

I n all of the Bible there's only one scene of a man kissing a woman.

There are plenty of children kissing parents and grandparents kissing grandchildren. There are kings kissing citizens and citizens kissing idols. There's also a hormone-enhanced couple who talk a mighty fine kiss: "Let him kiss me with the kisses of his mouth—for your love is more delightful than wine" (Song of Solomon 1:2). But if they ever did kiss, and I'm sure they did, they didn't kiss and tell.

The Bible's solitary kiss between a man and a woman took place at an isolated well in a pasture. There, "Jacob kissed Rachel" (Genesis 29:11). A month later Jacob asked for her hand in marriage and, because he had no money for the customary gift to her father, agreed to work seven years for him.

The low profile that romance takes in the Bible—with the notable exception of the passionate Song of Solomon—once fit quite nicely with my idea of romance, especially during my dating days and the early years of my marriage. Song of Solomon–style romance has never been natural for me, which may be partly why I once lost a perfectly fine girlfriend to a bald-headed insurance salesman. Two months later, still on the rebound and hurting, I met Linda. She had just moved to town.

It seems quite fitting that we met on Friday the thirteenth at a bad-luck-turnabout party. It also seems prophetic that we exchanged our first words over a game of Aggravation (she won the first game and I won the next), for within a year we would be married and experiencing the aggravating exchanges so common between newlyweds trying to adapt to one another's quirks.

The dearth of romance within me became most obvious on Valentine's Day, four months after I met Linda. I told Linda ahead of time that I had bought her a gift every woman wants. She knew that I was about finished with graduate school and was exploring editorial jobs throughout the country. So she expected an engagement ring.

That thought had never occurred to me.

I bought her a nice box of Russell Stover chocolates.

Linda tried to hide her disappointment, but the symptoms were obvious. Even to me. I watched her sadness crescendo as she took the box and then looked inside to find nothing but chocolate. For an instant, her face took on the dazed, expressionless stare of a battle-fatigued soldier retrieved from the front. Then she smiled—or tried to. The upward pull of her lips looked unnatural, contorted, painful.

"You were expecting a ring, weren't you?" I asked.

She nodded.

I hugged her and said that, when that time came, it

wouldn't be on a day everyone else was celebrating but on a day special to us.

Five weeks later I called her parents, who lived out of state and whom I had met briefly only twice. I asked for permission to propose marriage to their daughter. Graciously, they gave their blessing and agreed to keep the matter secret for a day. Early the next evening, Thursday, March 22, 1979, I drove Linda to an elegant restaurant that revolved twenty-eight floors above downtown Kansas City. There, on this thoroughly foreign turf and with my feet planted firmly nowhere near the ground, I would take my stand.

It was near the end of Happy Hour, and seated at a window table behind me was a middle-aged man talking to himself in a slurred English dialect. I was romantically challenged enough; I didn't need the added obstacle of having to time my proposal around this man's occasional bursts of chatter, let alone the continuing queries of Greg, our hovering server.

Yet I knew when the right moment arrived, thanks to singer Johnny Mathis. In soft and mellow tones that tumbled gently from speakers all over the restaurant, he began singing of love that would last "until the twelfth of never." The Happy Hour man was momentarily content and silent. Greg was gone with our salad plates (but he would soon return). Outside our window the colorful lights of the city beneath us began sparkling in the growing darkness that trailed the red and orange hues of the setting sun.

I needed only to speak the words. But what words? "Will you marry me?" seemed abrupt. I needed a transition. Something smooth. Something involving the song or the lights.

"See that tower over there?" I asked, pointing. It had

two blinking lights, one above the other.

"Yes."

"The top light is me, and the bottom light is you."

In retrospect, that was a pitiful transition and lousy theology. In the apostle Paul's lecture on marriage in Ephesians 5, the original Greek language has only one verb in the entire twelve-verse passage. And it's not the translated English verb indicating that women should be submissive to husbands. The Greek verb appears at the beginning, urging men and women to "submit to one another out of reverence for Christ" (Ephesians 5:21).

I should have skipped the transition.

"Will you?" I asked.

"Will I what?" Linda replied.

She was going to make me ask the whole question.

"Will you marry me?"

Four months later, and nine months after we first played Aggravation, we got married.

A Risky Business, Marriage

By this time, our new marriage had a fifty-fifty chance of surviving. For reasons uncertain, America's low divorce rates of 15 to 25 percent during the 1920s through the 1960s had blasted upward to about 50 percent in the 1970s—a rate that has since remained disturbingly steady in spite of a counter-surge of marriage therapists. Some experts blame the tragic divorce rates on the 1970 no-fault divorce law, which permits divorce even when one of the partners wants to try working out the problems.

Frankly, all the way through our dating and engagement I had questions about whether I wanted to spend the rest of my life with Linda. And after my Valentine's Day blunder, and certainly after my dumb remark about the lights on the tower, she should have had the same questions about me. But once we married, I didn't consider divorce. I had certainly read about divorce. And I had glimpsed it in the families of some folks I knew. But I had not yet experienced the reality of it through a close friend or through my own family. There were no divorces among my grandparents, parents, aunts, or uncles. These people, however, were married back in the days when *divorce* was a word describing people more abhorred than pitied. Linda and I were part of a new breed of spouse: the young and the restless. Anything could happen.

I've often heard about couples having the right chemistry, but I learned only recently that the chemistry involves real chemicals. When people fall in love they experience physical changes in their body: flushed skin, sweaty hands, heavy breathing. These symptoms are caused by the rush of dopamine, norepinephrine, and phenylethylamine—chemical cousins of amphetamines known as speed. The body builds up resistance to these natural drugs, which helps explain why the sense of infatuation eventually wears off. So perhaps we shouldn't be surprised by the finding of anthropologist Helen Fisher. After studying marriage in sixty-two cultures she discovered that divorce peaks at about the fourth year of marriage.

In my marriage, that would have been about the summer I pruned the weeping willow tree beside our backyard deck. I was perched thirty feet in the air, sawing away, when Linda came outside to empty her rubber dustpan. She looked up at her previously full willow, gasped at the blue sky, and ordered me to stop before I killed the tree. "It won't die," I said, still sawing. Linda tried to convince me otherwise, but I continued hacking one thick branch after another until Linda heaved the dustpan at me. Fortunately dustpans aren't very aerodynamic, and it missed me. Actually, Linda intended it as nothing more than a "warning shot over the bow," somewhat like the Coast Guard gives to uncooperative poachers.

I'd like to say I climbed down and rushed to apologize, but I nearly fell out of the tree laughing. I had never seen Linda that angry before, and the scene struck me as funny. It was a bit like picturing the *Leave It to Beaver* mom, June Cleaver, drop-kicking the milkman.

Linda withdrew to pout, and I sawed up one good cardiovascular workout. This wasn't what marriage experts today would describe as a healthy fight. It was the kind of fight that drives two people in opposite directions. Only one in five divorces are caused by adultery, says John Gottman, a professor of psychology at the University of Washington in Seattle. "Most marriages die with a whimper, as people turn away from one another, slowly growing apart."

Amazingly, some scientists who have been researching marriage for the past two decades claim they can predict with more than 90-percent accuracy whether a particular marriage will fail. These scientists base their predictions on an interview and a study of how the couple fights. In a marriage lab at the University of California at Berkeley, one of many such labs around the country, couples sit in straight-backed chairs and face each other. On cue, they begin a fifteen-minute argument on a topic of their choosing. The chairs are wired to measure how much they squirm. The subjects, too, are wired with monitoring devices on their chests and fingertips to gauge changes in pulse, blood pressure, temperature, and sweat. Video cameras display their faces on a split-screen TV in an adjoining room.

In one session witnessed and reported by a writer for *Health* magazine, a young doctor and his wife were on the lab's hot seats. The topic chosen by the doctor: the wife's closest friend had recently visited them for two months, leaving the doctor feeling abandoned.

"I become a second-class person in your life when she is around," the doctor says.

"Do you know why?" his wife asks.

"Because I feel slighted."

"No. It's because you don't try to make it work."

For five minutes, then ten, they go round and round. Then the wife rips into her husband, revealing in no uncertain terms why her friend is so important to her: "She gives me something that you don't. She appreciates me."

In silence, the doctor chews his lip and stares at the floor.

"She'll never come back because of you," the wife complains.

"That's fine."

The fifteen minutes is nearly over. "I'm getting sad," the wife says, wiping her eyes. "If she would come again, I'd have her stay in a minute."

"I wouldn't be there," the doctor retaliates.

"Go."

As if on cue, a lab worker knocks on the door. Fifteen minutes are up.

The husband laughs. "I knew that one would work," he says, congratulating himself on choosing such a hot topic.

But it's not the topic of arguments that serves as an accurate predictor of divorce, say researchers. All couples argue about much the same things: money, sex, and dead carp or living company that hang around past a long weekend. It doesn't even matter how much or how loudly a couple argues. Marriages can endure whether the spouses are calm, hotheaded, or argument dodgers. What matters, say researchers, is that the couple shares the same fighting style and finds a balance in the good and bad moments between them. In fact, couples satisfied with their marriages share about five kind moments for every moment of anger or complaint.

In my case, that's one "I love you," one "How sweet!" one wink, one favorite meal prepared, and one quick peck on the cheek for every primal scream such as "Get outta that tree!"

The good news for couples who can't match those numbers or who have conflicting styles of fighting is that we human beings are adaptable. We can learn how to change our fighting tactics, and we can discover the importance of kindness. This awareness, along with the soaring divorce rate, is spurring more and more cities throughout the country to require couples to take marriage classes before being issued a marriage license.

Linda and I had to learn our lessons the hard way. We're self-taught. Early in our marriage, I was skilled at stating my position clearly, firmly, and, on occasion, loudly. Linda was skilled at exiting Stage Right, crying.

One common complaint of mine had to do with housekeeping. I liked things neat, and Linda didn't mind clutter. In fact, it seemed she had a phobia about uncovered flat surfaces in the house—they all had to be covered, if not with decorations, with folded layers of laundry waiting to be mended, teetering towers of receipts longing to be filed, and bulging bags of craft knickknack-paddy-wacks hoping someday to be assembled. I especially hated scattered stacks of paperwork on the only dining table in our house. There was no rest for the weary eye, no clutter-free respite amid the junkyard.

I dubbed the stacks "Linda piles." Linda would move them on request, though I seldom knew where. I do know, however, they kept popping up like the molehills that erupted in our backyard one summer. I killed the mole with a steel trap. Solving the problem inside the house took more effort. I had to build an attic.

And even that wasn't enough. The stacks gradually returned. Eventually, we worked out a compromise. We agreed to fewer stacks and that they be located in less intrusive locations, such as the bedroom closet. The "Linda pile" of receipts, coupons, and mail on the dinner table was moved to behind the lower left door inside the china cabinet. Linda sorts through it about once a week.

Beyond learning to compromise, we learned to talk more. Linda became more articulate in stating her position when we disagreed. Once, when I was in a persistent vegetative state and behaving as though I had cream of mushroom soup for brains, she wrote me a five-page letter. I still have it.

The letter is dated January 17, 1988. Rebecca was two-and-a-half years old, and Bradley was five months. This was a wearying, sleep-deprived, grumpy moment in my life—not one of the embraceable moments but one of the erasable. It was just a week earlier that the entire family had come down with the flu, sending Linda into the hospital and leaving me home alone with the kids. It was during the lingering months when Bradley, even healthy, demanded incredible attention in daylight and darkness. The exchanges between Linda and me during those months were not quite in the ratio of five kind moments for every one angry moment. More like the opposite.

"Steve," she wrote, "I really don't feel like putting 'Dear' in front of your name tonight." And then with honest candor and compassionate pleading, she said that she feared for our marriage. She admitted that the times were difficult for both of us. She praised me for the many chores I did to help her, even naming them one by one, but she said that my repeated complaining had left her feeling that I didn't love her or even care about her. She said that she believed God wanted us to work things out, but that "tonight, I'm on a narrow ledge and can go either way. Please help me! I need some love from you."

With the following paragraph she closed her handwritten note, inscribed on stationery beautifully embossed and cut with the design of flowers scaling a wooden lattice: "I guess in all, I'm trying to say please help me rekindle the fire I had for you when we first met. I fear it is slowly being snuffed out, although it's not entirely your fault; it's mine too. Please, help me. I sure do need you right now. Linda."

She didn't sign it with the word *Love*.

But her love was powerfully evident in her very act of writing. She wanted our marriage. She wanted my love. She wanted me. I was jarred by the letter. With simple and unassuming eloquence, Linda not only had summed up exactly what was damaging our relationship but had assessed the extent of that damage—an assessment that came as a horrifying and painful shock to me. I hadn't realize she was thinking about leaving. Further, in her unpretentious pleading, she revealed what we needed to do to save our relationship. She wasn't as specific as today's marriage researchers who suggest five kind moments for every unkind one, but she did ask for more kindness.

I had fallen into the common trap of taking my loved one for granted and treating her worse than I treated my friends—worse, in fact, than I treated strangers. I was more likely to compliment my barber on a nice job than to praise my wife for anything.

Linda got what she asked for.

The thought of suddenly losing her was a powerful motivator for me. Her letter became a turning point in our marriage, which is why I kept it. Perhaps one day I'll have my children read it as part of a homespun, school-of-hard-knocks course on marriage.

A Worthy Risk, Marriage

With divorce rates as high as they are, and with the chemistry of love eventually wearing off as it does, some people make a strong case for not getting married. Instead, they float from one unfettered relationship to another and from one fading chemical attraction to a new and hopefully more potent chemical allure.

Please don't hear what I'm about to say as an attack on single adults. I was single until I was nearly twenty-seven years old. And I know that God uses single adults in situations too time-consuming and long-term for married people, who are busy caring for their own families. As a young and lonely seminary student who had moved far from home, I was treated like a son by a never-married Christian gentleman in the church I began attending. He introduced me to city sights, restaurants, and friends. He was then and is now a gifted encourager well known for his compassionate ministry.

In spite of the fact that God's kingdom has plenty of room for both singles and married people, most human beings need a mate. A variety of recent medical studies have reached the same conclusion about humanity that God reached about Adam: "It is not good for the man to be alone" (Genesis 2:18).

Married people live longer than single people. In one study among middle-aged men, researchers from the University of California discovered that during a ten-year span, unmarried men were twice as likely to die as married men. Loneliness apparently wasn't the distinguishing factor because unmarried men living with companions also suffered the same lower survival rates as those who lived alone. There's something physically healthy about being married. What it is, no one knows for certain. There are probably many factors. One might be the loving care they receive. It makes a difference in rabbits. In a study of rabbits fed a high-cholesterol diet, a group that got extra care and loving strokes showed a 60-percent reduction in artery blockages. For people with high cholesterol, a good marriage might actually be better than oatmeal.

In a fifteen-year study of nearly a million women, those who never married were more likely to commit suicide than were married women. And among married women, the more children they had, the less likely they were to take their own lives.

Aside from the obvious advantages of marriage—hugs, kisses, companionship, help, and descendants, to name a few— there's the surprising extra perk that it tends to keep us on the planet longer.

Until the Twelfth of Never

I've heard of people who say they found and married their soul mate, the one person who, more than any other, mystically and almost magically makes them feel complete. I've experienced the emotion only vicariously, thanks to Hollywood and films such as *Sleepless in Seattle*. I've never thought of Linda as my one and only soul mate.

I have tried.

There have been shared moments of potent tenderness when I would look deeply into her eyes, which are said to be windows to the human soul. On occasion I've even said, "I just want to look into your eyes for a while." I was searching for a feeling: a sense of spiritual connection, a magical moment of Hollywood romance, or at least a chemical reaction. Instead, I found only patience. She would allow me to look, and she would devotedly look back, but after a few seconds the experience became an uncomfortable exercise: four staring eyeballs trying not to blink.

I used to wonder what my life would have been like if I had married a soul mate. What if I had not felt time-pressured into deciding on Linda before taking a job in another state? It would be quite possible for me to talk myself into thinking that I settled for second best. And I know better than anyone that Linda could certainly think the same of me. But we made a promise in the sight of God that we would spend our lives together. God himself sealed our marriage, as he does the marriages of all couples. "The two will become one flesh," Jesus said. "They are no longer two, but one. Therefore what God has joined together, let man not separate" (Mark 10:8-9). If God united us, he certainly stands with us. And if God is with us, how can that be second best?

In the last few years I've seen "till death us do part." Standing in the church lobby, I've held tightly to both hands of a new widow, who burst into tears when I spoke her husband's name and told her how sorry I was to hear of his death. I've passed new widowers walking alone in crowded hallways, on their way from Sunday school class to worship service—a weekly route they had traveled for years with their wives. I try to catch their eyes and greet them, but often they are looking down and sweep past without receiving a smile or a word.

The saddest and most lost-looking widower I ever saw was Dr. Ralph Earle, the fellow church member I mentioned in chapter one. Chairman of the committee of scholars who translated the *New International Version* of the Bible, Ralph had been married to Mabel for sixty-three years. She died from painful injuries suffered in a fire in her kitchen.

I vividly remember seeing Ralph sitting in a pew on his first Sunday back after the funeral. He was surrounded by his family, who had come to take him to live with them out of state. Ralph looked beyond lost; he looked as though he weren't there, as though his soul had fled in pursuit of his love. Mabel had been an important part of all aspects of his life, including his scholarly achievements. I remember his saying once that when he had a critical issue coming up among committee members working on the *NIV,* Mabel spent the lunch time with him in fervent prayer. For Ralph and Mabel, a lifetime had passed in a moment, and a thousand years would have seemed but a day. But with Mabel gone, life for the esteemed scholar must have seemed unbearable, with each day like a thousand years. He died two months later.

I don't know what it's like to live with a love for sixty-three years; in fact, I'll never know unless I manage to disappoint my health insurance company by outliving my projected life span. But I know what it's been like to live with Linda for nineteen years: it's been a forty-five-second roller coaster ride with all the exhilaration, terror, relief, and calm that one soul could stand.

I have no reason to believe that the next nineteen years will pass more slowly. Fact is, I expect the ride to pick up speed. That's because it has been my experience that the more years I pile on, the more time is compressed and the faster life goes. In what may seem like just another few seconds, it could be me sitting in the pew surrounded by my children and grandchildren. It could be me staring out of focus, wishing I could once again search Linda's patient eyes. Wondering if I had shown her the kindness to thank her half as much as I had thanked my barber or the grocer at the checkout counter. Wanting one more chance to tell her she has been a good wife and has filled my life with joy.

But by then, in the seeming blink of an eye, it will be too late.

"What is your life?" the New Testament writer James asks. "You are a mist that appears for a little while and then vanishes" (James 4:14). Too soon, Linda will be gone. So will I, for that matter. This is the moment that God has given us to declare in words spoken and in feelings expressed that "I am my lover's and my lover is mine" (Song of Solomon 6:3).

CHAPTER 6

A Moment
for Your Family

My days are swifter than a runner....
They skim past like boats of papyrus.
JOB 9:25-26

"You care more about your writing than about us."

Rebecca was seven years old when she popped her head into my home office and announced the verdict.

My mouth dropped and my fingers lay frozen on the computer keyboard. I had made it a practice not to write at home during the evenings or weekends unless Rebecca and Bradley were off playing with neighbor kids or sleeping. Since they were playing and Linda was relaxing, I had decided to work a bit on a freelance assignment. Rebecca's words surprised and hurt me.

"What makes you say that?" I asked.

Perhaps the shocked expression on my face and the serious tone of my voice caught her off guard, for she responded with a lie.

"Mom said it."

My eyebrows arched high into my forehead an instant before I sprang from my chair.

"Just kidding," she said. And off she streaked into the backyard.

Linda confirmed she had said nothing of the kind. Our little teaser was experimenting with another technique for getting my attention. It worked. I went straight to the backyard, picked up a soccer ball, and played those kids into a sweat.

Why Family Time Is Important

The time I spend with my wife and children is important. I know this for many reasons. One piece of evidence in particular became deeply etched into my spirit when we took my mother to the West Virginia valley that had once been her home. I wanted my wife and children to see where I had spent so many happy weekend and summer getaways, visiting my grandparents.

Their home was a simple one, an unpainted, two-story wood house beside a one-lane dirt road. There was no driveway, just a wide spot in the road for family and guests to park. Surrounding the small yard was a chicken-wire fence, supported by vertical stakes and diagonal poles that my grandfather had cut from saplings. As a youngster, I would dash through the gateway and down the short, dirt path into the house, where hugs and kisses awaited me. Afterward, there were chickens to chase, hound dogs to pet, woods to explore, grapevines to swing on, a shallow bedrock creek to wade in, a cow to stalk, beehives to stir (with well-thrown rocks), a one-seat outhouse to check for spiders, and enough sharp and heavy steel tools in the blacksmith shop that it's a wonder I reached adulthood with all my fingers and toes.

Mom was born and raised in that place. Many of her childhood memories are mine as well, for we scampered about the same hills, got stung by the same family of bees, and learned to love Granny's buckwheat pancakes topped with a chunk of homemade butter then smothered with hot, skillet-browned flour gravy.

Some thirty years had passed when we returned with Mom. There was still a wide spot on the one-lane dirt road at the base of the hill that leads to Kingwood. But the house built by Grandpap's dad had long since been abandoned, then set ablaze before it could decay and crumble, possibly hurting children at play or wanderers spending the night. The yard that had so kindly entertained generations of children had become a thick and monstrous weed patch that towered high above our heads. Weeds taller than Iowa corn were all we could see as we stood along the roadside. Mom and I wanted to walk onto the property, touching at least the land and the foundation of the house, perhaps to make our memories more real. But with one step off the road we would have been engulfed in bristles and briars.

I tried to point out to Linda and the kids where the house had stood and how the wedge-shaped yard sat on a tiny, slanted plateau thirty feet above the creek that we could hear splashing over rocks in the distance. But all anyone could see was the wall of weeds and my mother silently crying before them.

I don't know for certain why she cried. But something about this valley was worth crying over. I believe it had to do with what happened there—with the raising of a family.

Someday, when Mom and Dad are gone and the Akron home I was raised in has become a four-lane thoroughfare to Rolling Acres Mall or a parking lot for a Laundromat, I'll likely go there, too. Perhaps I'll park my car and stand awhile.

Maybe I'll remember the evening the bat flew in, and we boys took turns chasing it with a broom. And there was the night my year-younger brother, Cliff, plotted to scare me by hiding under my bed. I saw his socked foot sticking out just beyond the shadows, discerned his plan, and hatched one of my own. Quickly, I dressed in my nightclothes, shut the bedroom door, turned out the lights, and climbed into bed. When the room was blacker than black and stiller than still, in those long and fearful moments when children's eyes become worthless and their ears magnify the slightest creak, I emptied my lungs with the exclamation, "The devil's under the bed!"

Two loud, rhythmic bumps followed.

The first was Cliff's head striking the bed railing as he bolted up in his rush to escape. The second was his torso crashing into the door, normally kept open. He screamed one continuous "Ah-h-h-h-h-h" all the way down the stairs to Mom, leaving behind the sound trail of a person falling off of a mountain. Since he was terrified and inconsolable, Mom made me sleep with him that night.

Surely I'll remember Dad wrestling all five of his kids at the same time, positioning himself on all fours, like a collegiate wrestler, and challenging us to keep him from standing. We three boys would pile onto his back or wrap ourselves around his legs, while our two sisters followed Mom's coaching and tickled him in the ribs or twisted his nose.

As I stand beside my car and try to picture the home in which all this happened, maybe I'll respond the way Mom did at the weed patch. If I do, I'll blame it on the genetic programming she passed along to me.

We're not limited to personal insights about how important the family is. The evidence is all around us.

Consider the Statistics

Cornell University research shows that a two-parent home is a kid's best protection against dropping out of school, using drugs, marrying young, getting a divorce, or living in poverty. Fatherless kids are twice as likely to become school dropouts. Seventy percent of kids in reform school grew up in a single- or no-parent setting.

Single-parent homes weren't a big problem when I was a kid in the 1950s. About 95 percent of children had both parents. But now, less than 60 percent do. Sociologists say that more than half of today's kids will probably spend at least part of their childhood with just one parent. More than half.

Look at MTV

Silhouettes thrash against the wall. A figure of a child raises his arms to protect himself as a huge shadow pounds him wildly, delivering blow upon blow. The scene is from a music video called "Father." It's meant to portray the beatings that rapper LL Cool J says he got from his stepfather.

As the beatings play on, LL raps a chorus equally unrelenting, repeated over and over: "All I ever wanted. All I ever needed. Was a father." A real father. Approachable. Loving. Committed.

When LL grew up, he met a young lady who gave birth to his children. One day his son asked, "Daddy, are you going to marry Mommy?"

"That was deep to listen to," said LL. "That told me he was yearning for a family unit and how important it was."

Daddy did marry Mommy.

Study Recent American History

President John F. Kennedy was known more for his philandering than for his love of wife and children. But when the Cuban missile crisis arrived midway through his thousand-day presidency, when the United States teetered perilously close to nuclear war with Cuba and the Soviet Union, President Kennedy's thoughts turned toward home, says biographer Edward Klein. And those thoughts affected his decisions in ways so crucial that I may never be able to vote for a presidential candidate who has no children.

Kennedy decided that, instead of launching a preemptive air strike against Cuba to destroy the nuclear missiles that the Soviets deployed only ninety miles from Florida, he would order a naval blockade of the island. Why such restraint?

"If it weren't for the children," the president later told his friend, Dave Powers, "it would be so easy to press the button!"

A bit later that day, Powers went to the family quarters in the White House to deliver a folder to the president. The living room was dimly lit and the president was speaking softly. Powers thought the president was on the phone. Stepping closer, he saw that four-year-old Caroline was sitting on her father's lap, listening to him read from a storybook.

"I thought of what he had been saying to me," Powers said. "I got the strangest feeling. I handed him the papers and got out of there as fast as I could. I was all choked up."

Read the Bible

Unfortunately, the Bible's evidence is found mostly in tragic examples of what happens when people ignore needs in their families. Jacob was so out of touch with most of his children that he saw no problem in showing blatant favoritism to his young son Joseph. When Jacob's older sons had all they could take, they sold Joseph to slave traders and told their father that the boy had been eaten by a wild animal.

In another painful example, King David had at least six wives and a complex family life filled with rivalries, abuse, and bitterness. For instance, one son raped his half-sister. And when David failed to punish the young man, the victim's full-brother, Absalom, not only killed the rapist but later launched a coup against David. Absalom was killed execution-style in the revolt, though David had given specific orders that he be spared. When David heard of his son's death, he was shaken. In anguish he cried out, "O my son Absalom! My son, my son Absalom! If only I had died instead of you!" (2 Samuel 18:33). Any parent who has ever loved a child can understand the grief that David suffered for the rest of his life.

Israel's long history is packed so full of family heartache and tragedy that a sage once felt compelled to give this advice to the young men he was teaching: "He who brings trouble on his family will inherit only wind" (Proverbs 11:29).

Searching for Quality Time

Most of us paying attention know that family time is important. But when time is short, many rely on quality time—the notion that it isn't how much time you spend with your family but how well you spend the time.

The first time I heard of quality time, a preacher was doing the talking. Though I'm not a preacher, I was sitting in on his seminar for preachers in the area. Stout and thirtyish, the articulate gentleman was advising his colleagues how to strike a balance between the demands of church and family. It was the blind leading the blind. Ever-on-call preachers seem seldom home for any reason other than sleep or an early evening shave.

"I can't spend much time with my family," the minister admitted, "but we have quality time. We'll sometimes meet in the mall and go for a walk."

Excuse me. I've walked in malls with my family. There are plenty of adjectives I could use to describe that time, but *quality* is not one of them. Even the health benefits of the walk are lost in damage done to stomach lining, psyche, and budget. Kids make covert attempts to touch expensive breakables. Grown-ups linger over drably colored merchandise, which somehow triggers children to release a powerful fidgeting hormone that induces tempestuous convulsions and tantrums. Fashion-conscious kids win over one adult and plead a case for impulse buying, while the other adult, the keeper of the budget, picks up the pace of the walk.

"Quality time" is a vague phrase. People can't agree on what it means, only what it does. Time-pressured adults feel better if they can convince themselves that the few minutes they give their family is quality time. To some, quality time means scheduling part of each day for the family, just as we do with projects at work. "OK, kids, it's bedtime in fifteen minutes, so let's hear a report of your day. Hurry up now, let's get on with it." A pint-size staff meeting is not quality time.

For others, it means being in the general vicinity of the family. A former coworker of mine once bragged about how buying a laptop computer improved his family life by letting him do evening work in the living room, where his kids could see him. But if being in the general vicinity is quality time, then I've bonded with beasts at the zoo. Our kids and spouse need more than a grown body making irritating tapping sounds in the corner. They need eye contact, small talk, laughing, touching, pecks on the cheek, opinions exchanged, sadness shared, fears calmed. All these experiences build relationships, helping people get to know one another and fall in love, then helping them grow together instead of apart.

For still others, quality time is being available in times of distress. A friend of the late William S. Paley, founder and chairman of CBS, wrote a eulogy about this man who devoted his life to pursuing wealth and power. Paley, said the friend, wasn't the kind of guy who would go to his kids' Little League games, but when they needed him, he was there.

Well, they needed him at the games. What greater distress is there than looking down the barrel of a fast ball, fired by a freckle faced kid who popped the helmet off the last batter? Kids remember when their parents are no-shows. And they feel the disappointment for the rest of their lives.

I ran track in junior high school. I remember walking alone to the school track. I remember Mom driving me to races at other schools, dropping me off, and picking me up afterward. But I have no memory of anyone in my family ever watching me race. Dad worked second shift, and Mom had four younger kids to care for. So I know they had tremendous time pressures. Still, I wish they could have been there. I wish I could have heard them yelling my name, "Go, Steve!" Once, in a close race, I heard a friend of mine do that for me. She yelled so loud I could hear her from the opposite side of the field. I won that race, to the coach's amazement.

Now I'm the parent. I've been to more baseball practices

and games in the last three years than Cal Ripken. Well, almost. Then there's basketball. And soccer. Take it from me, our kids need us then. A strikeout. A foul called for traveling. A smash-mouth coach shredding his players during time-outs. It never fails: my kid turns and looks at me. I have two hand signals, both to encourage. A fist to my heart in a salute means, "It's OK. Don't let it bother you." A huge and invisible smile line pulled across my chest means, "Great play! We're talking athletic scholarship!"

Oh, yeah. I scream. Not the angry stuff. Just an applause from the vocal cords. Whether it's my kid or a teammate, when I see a hit, a basket, or a goal, I yell out the kid's name. (You get to know the whole team when you go to the practices.) As a veteran of several seasons, I've noticed that kids who have parents giving them strong and positive support generally develop their playing skills more quickly than others and enjoy the game more. As expressed by the ten-year-old son of Bill Galston, former policy adviser for President Bill Clinton, "baseball's not fun when there's no one there to applaud you." Convinced, Galston resigned his time-guzzling job and returned to teaching.

The family needs us when they're off the playing field too. Or in my daughter's case with piano recitals, when she's off the stage. Some would argue that quality time with Rebecca would be attending her recitals—with a video camera, of course. But is the recital a higher-quality investment of my time than driving her to piano lessons, then suffering with her as she fights her way through a gauntlet of sharps and flats?

On the drive home from lessons a few weeks ago, Rebecca felt bitterly discouraged, ready to quit. But I told her that as she played her recital piece for the instructor, I was sitting behind her smiling and enjoying the absolutely beautiful music. (It's true, I was.) I said that with her music she has the power to make others feel as happy as she made me feel. Rebecca was startled. Even speechless, for a change. She paused, then her face blossomed with delight. She has been practicing with more gusto ever since. I don't know how long my compliment will energize her, but when her zeal wanes I hope her mother or I will be around to give her a booster shot.

"Quality time is just a way of deluding ourselves into short-changing our children," says Ronald Levant, a psychologist at Harvard Medical School. "Children need vast amounts of parental time." Lotte Bailyn agrees. She's a professor at MIT's Sloan School of Management, and she leads a team that helps companies become more productive and make better use of their employees' time. "Quality time belongs at work," she says. "Quantity time belongs with the family."

Stephen Covey's best-selling book *The Seven Habits of Highly Effective People* dispensed advice about how to be successful in business. It sold more than twelve million copies and was on the best-seller lists for more than five years. Working late was not one of his recommended seven habits. He has since written a book called *The Seven Habits of Highly Effective Families*. When a *Newsweek* magazine writer called at 7 P.M. to interview him about it, he was disturbed.

"I can't believe you're there," he said. "It's late. Do you have a family?"

I love what these experts are saying. According to other experts, however, I've been programmed to agree. That's because I'm a boomer raised in the 1950s, when countless dads were emotionally distant from their kids and always working— at the job, on the house, in the yard, under the car. We boomers who are now fathers, say sociologists, are raising our kids in opposition to how we were raised. We were raised, to a great extent, without our dads around. So we've been making dog-gone sure that our kids don't have to grow up with the same sense of deprivation. And we're hoping that if some television network picks our kids out of a crowd someday and points a TV camera at them, they'll yell, "Hi, Dad. I love you."

In my house, as a youngster, Dad's absence was especially noticeable because he worked second shift. He left the house at around 3:30 in the afternoon (about the time school ended), and he didn't get home from the factory until just before midnight (long past our bedtime). He chose this shift; it wasn't forced on him. Perhaps he preferred the shift because it helped him reach his top priorities: keeping a roof over our heads, food on the table, and a car that would run. He slept when we slept. He performed his never-ending household maintenance and tinkered on his projects while we were at school. And he worked in the comparative peace of a high-decibel machine shop while we five kids, all born within seven years of each other, tested the mettle that mothers are made of.

Friday nights were a treat for me because Mom let me wait up for Dad. When he got home, I'd open his lunch box and generally find a candy bar or some other snack he had bought off the lunch wagon that made rounds in the shop. I'd claim the treat, then fix Dad a bowl of cereal if he was hungry. Once, I remember opening the kitchen cabinet while asking, "Want some Wheaties?" It was his favorite.

"Yeah," he answered.

"We don't have any."

The box was gone, but I hadn't discovered this until after I made the offer. Dad gave me the oddest look, which was in no way related to a smile. Perhaps he was wondering if I had suddenly entered a disrespectful stage of childhood. But he accepted my explanation along with a glass of milk, and we watched Johnny Carson's *Tonight Show* together.

Except for the three summer months when we kids were free of school, weekends were about the only time we got to see Dad. But even then, he was usually fixing something. If not for us, for someone else. He could fix just about anything, especially cars.

Don't get me wrong: Dad didn't ignore his kids. He took us sledding on Firestone hill. I remember because he broke my sled. He got it airborne on a bump, and the steel runners couldn't handle his touchdown. Dad often whisked the whole family off to our grandparents' on weekend mini-vacations. There, among the rolling hills and fields of West Virginia, he would let us take turns sitting on his lap and steering the chopped-down Chrysler that Grandpa had turned into a frumpy, post-apocalyptic tractor. Once a year he took us on a camping vacation. He later admitted that he hated camping (which came as a surprise to me), but that we camped because we couldn't afford hotels. No loss as far as I'm concerned. Some of the best memories of my childhood are from those camping trips to mountains and beaches.

My regret isn't that Dad wasn't around but that he wasn't around more. He says he now regrets it too. I believe him because he goes far out of his way to spend time with his adult children and with his grandkids. In his seventies, he still drives the eight hundred miles each year to see us in Kansas City. (We can't talk him into flying.)

I've learned from my Dad's regrets and from the loss I still feel from my growing-up days. I know that childhood comes and goes in the blink of an eye and that, once it's gone, it's gone forever. Even more alarming is that my kids are changing every day, physically, mentally, emotionally. What's more, every day is irreplaceable. So at workday's end, I belong to my family. That may mean fixing supper, helping with homework, playing soccer in the backyard, double-dribbling in the driveway, losing hard-fought Nintendo and chess games to Bradley, listening to Rebecca's impromptu piano and vocal concerts in the living room, or enjoying a meal out with my wife.

What's so important about being with them? It was about 9:30 on a Sunday night in February. Bradley, then four years old, had taken a late nap, so he wasn't ready to go to bed when Rebecca did. Linda was working night shift at the hospital, in her part-time job as a pediatric nurse, so it was just Bradley and I alone together.

In a few days I was going to be in Israel, on a three-week assignment. Though I was excited about the trip I was already missing my family. I took Bradley to bed with me that night. I cuddled up close to him and asked his permission to lay my head against his shoulder. He said it was OK. He was warm and tiny, only thirty-four pounds. Rib-bulging skinny, like I was at his age.

"I love you, Bradley," I whispered.

"I love you, too," he said, mimicking my soft tone.

"Will you always love me?"

"Yes. I will love you even when you go to heaven."

Mist filled my eyes then dampened the pillow, for I knew that, if the cycle of life runs its usual course, I will one day have to leave him alone with his memory of me. If he experiences love when he thinks of me, I will have left the world the greatest legacy of all.

"Thank you," I said.

A few minutes later, he was asleep. But I lay awake for some time.

CHAPTER 7

A Moment
for the Helpless

If a man shuts his ears to the cry of the poor,
he too will cry out and not be answered.
PROVERBS 21:13

On that mid-September Saturday when the world buried Mother Teresa, I was lying on a beige couch in my suburban living room, reading a 526-page book titled *Wealth: Enhancement and Preservation.*

When I punched on the TV remote to catch news at the top of the hour, there she was, lying in a white casket and being pulled on a gun carriage behind a green military troop truck. Inside the truck were nuns and soldiers, seated face-to-face like allied warriors on the road to battle. Military police in red-plumed turbans held back thousands who lined the streets along the three-mile route from St. Thomas' Church, in the heart of Calcutta's slum, to Netaji Indoor Stadium, where the best seats in the house were an odd assortment of spongy armchairs and sofas that looked to be borrowed for the occasion. In them sat presidents, queens, and the First Lady. The power of that moment—of holding on my chest a book about wealth while watching the funeral of a woman who had devoted herself to the poorest of the poor—has been forever seared into my mind.

I live with the memory that, when I first heard of President John F. Kennedy's assassination, I was on my way home from grade school and laughing; suddenly, some older kids scolded me for not showing respect. I remember, too, watching television coverage of the shuttle *Challenger* explosion while rocking my baby daughter to sleep and trying not to cry so loudly that I would awaken her. And now added to these is the memory of watching Mother Teresa's funeral while I pondered ways to make more money and reclined in a seat more comfortable than the best available to world dignitaries there.

It occurred to me to close the book and never open it again. But I punched off the remote and read on. The book had been given to me by a financial planner whom Linda and I were thinking about hiring. He was one of the book's authors, a young Christian who specializes in developing financial strategies for people in the health-care community. I justified my reading that afternoon by reminding myself that each year this financial planner organizes teams of doctors and nurses, taking them to developing nations to perform free surgeries. Besides, I was just trying to make sure our kids have some money for college and that Linda and I have food and shelter during our retirement.

Yet the disparity between Mother Teresa's world in the heart of Calcutta's slum and my world in the heart of America's breadbasket lingered with me as I read, and troubles me even now. I don't know how to correct this inequity on a global scale. But I suspect it all starts with achieving in my personal life a balance between self-preservation and compassion.

God must have seen that we humans err on the side of taking doggone good care of ourselves because his messengers never nudge us in that direction. Instead, they repeatedly prod us toward compassion: "Do not be hardhearted or tightfisted toward your poor brother" (Deuteronomy 15:7); "Seek justice, encourage the oppressed. Defend the cause of the fatherless, plead the case of the widow" (Isaiah 1:17); "If anyone has material possessions and sees his brother in need but has no pity on him, how can the love of God be in him?" (1 John 3:17).

The Helpless Among Us

I don't live in Calcutta. But there *are* helpless people within my reach.

Kids in Danger

Martin Luther King, Jr., had a dream. In honor of Dr. King's birthday, a Kansas City school asked its first graders what their dreams were. Their dreams were then posted on the walls of Kansas University Medical Center for all to see. Some signed their dreams, others did not. Here is what some of them wrote:

> "I have a dream of no more taking drugs or robbing banks or kicking kids."—Daniel

> "I have a dream that one day people would all get together and be friends and not judge people by the way their skin is. But people still do."

> "I have a dream that everyone has a place to live."
>
> —Nadreka

"I have a dream that nobody would have a gun and that nobody would kill each other and that nobody would kill my uncle."

"I have a dream that all children are loved."

—Cheryl

It was about eight o'clock on an August evening when a neighbor girl called my daughter and asked if she could come over to our house to play. I told Rebecca no, reminding her that we had been gone all day and were trying to get the house ready for my parents, who were arriving the next day. Rebecca talked with her friend awhile longer, then paused to ask me again. But this time Rebecca explained that her friend was scared because her parents were yelling at each other. The little girl's mother had locked herself in the bedroom, and the father had punched one hole in the wall and another through the bedroom door.

For that moment in time, Rebecca's friend was an orphan—emotionally abandoned, terrified, and possibly in danger. Just as our instincts tell us when to run for safety, our spirits tell us when to help another. A few minutes later, Rebecca's friend arrived. Bradley and I played kickball with Rebecca and her friend well into the darkness. We then walked the girl home and made sure her parents had calmed down. The dad was sitting quietly on the couch while the mom frantically cleaned house.

Neighbors in Need
We've lived in our house for about eighteen years; during that time my wife has gone flying out our front door on medical emergencies more times than I can count. Linda has

covered all four directions of the compass.

East: a neighbor pinned between a car and a garage when his jack slipped.

West: a child with a throbbing ear.

North: an elderly friend dying of cancer and gasping for breath.

South: a baby girl with a lung disorder, who had turned blue from oxygen deprivation. Since Linda is a pediatric nurse, the paramedics and parents were all relieved when Linda offered to ride in the ambulance to the hospital.

That's just a sampling of Linda's work as a neighborhood nurse. I, on the other hand, am a writer and an editor. None of my neighbors has ever called me frantically pleading, "Quick, bring your laptop!" Which is a good thing, since I don't have one. But when I keep my eyes and ears open, even I can sometimes discover ways to be a helpful neighbor.

Once, sitting on the wooden swing on my backyard deck, I watched pantomime theater across our chain link fence. There were words, but I couldn't hear them. It's probably for the best. The air smelled of freshly mown grass as the man of the house, Bill Darrah, stood beside his silent mower. His wife, Linda, was doing some kind of war dance in front of him, stabbing the sky with fingers and fists, stomping the ground, and making faces as though reenacting the sacrifice of a young virgin whose heart was being cut out to assure victory. Just a few years older than I, Bill is a workaholic mechanic who had suffered a heart attack a few months earlier. I spoke briefly of him in chapter four.

When I saw him cutting the grass that afternoon, I figured he had been given the OK by his doctor. Otherwise, his wife would have mowed it for him, as she had done—red faced, huffing and puffing—in the weeks earlier. But his wife's dance upon the lawn and his droopy-head posture of shame made it clear that he had certainly not been released for mower duty.

The next time I gassed up my own lawnmower, I took a walk next door. I told my neighbor, who has helped me split logs, tutored me in car repair, and given my kids extra candy at Halloween, that if it would be OK with him I would cut his lawn each time I cut mine, until the doctor released him. Who knows, I may have prevented another heart attack—his wife's, if not his. I had only a small window of opportunity for showing compassion to this neighbor, just a few weeks. Though I hate cutting grass, I'll never regret doing this for him because I knew that he and his wife needed the help.

On the other hand, I'll forever regret one moment on a cool and rainy spring afternoon when, as a college student working at a gas station, I decided against loaning my jacket to a frail and elderly man who was walking, shirt-sleeved, to the grocery store to redeem the deposit of an armload of empty pop bottles. I think of him when preachers read Jesus' parable about helping the needy: "I needed clothes and you clothed me, I was sick and you looked after me. . . . I tell you the truth, whatever you did for one of the least of these brothers of mine, you did for me" (Matthew 25:36, 40).

A Loved One in Crisis

Sometimes we don't have to leave our house to find a helpless person. On the Saturday night when the Cleveland Indians were leading the Florida Marlins 1-0 early in the first game of the 1997 World Series, I got a call from the hospital where Linda works. She had tripped over a phone cord and dived, left shoulder first, onto the cement floor. The X-rays revealed that her shoulder and upper arm were shattered in at least seven places.

Linda is left-handed. It would take nearly three months before she could return to work, even on restricted duty as a unit secretary instead of her more physically demanding job as a nurse.

Life changed immediately for both of us. Suddenly I was in charge of everything, which required bouncing around like a pinball from six in the morning until ten at night, when I would drop, lifeless, into bed. This schedule wasn't like being a single parent but like being a single parent struggling to keep the commitments made by two parents.

For our kids alone, each week I had to be at a total of four basketball practices, two soccer practices, one soccer game, and one piano lesson. Linda, who quickly became known to our son as "One Arm," couldn't dress herself, curl her hair, or even open the medicine bottles. She certainly couldn't fix meals, write checks to pay the bills, or go grocery shopping. Fortunately, because of my home office set-up, I could keep tabs on her throughout the day and interrupt my work as needed for such tasks as ushering her through the bewildering maze of doctors and bureaucrats that worker's compensation has erected.

About a week after the accident I came zooming down our hallway, headed toward some now unremembered chore in the kitchen, when I saw Linda sitting on the living room couch, crying. She was still on heavy doses of pain pills and sleeping a lot. Under her fluffy aqua housecoat she wore a gray mini–straitjacket that was Velcro-strapped around her torso and broken arm to secure the arm in place against her lower chest; the bone breaks were too high for a cast. On her left bicep she bore a hideous green and purple bruise that covered nearly all the skin from her inside elbow to her shoulder. The outside of her arm was death black.

Though this misery was hidden beneath the fluffy robe, sit-ting on top was a head that gave it all away. Linda's face hung flaccidly, and her black and graying hair was scattered about in dangling strings and knotted clumps that looked oddly remi-niscent of Andy Warhol, Don King, and a tumbleweed.

"Why are you crying?" I asked.

"I feel worthless."

I'd like to say that I took a few minutes to discuss the matter with her. But I didn't. On the plus side, at least I didn't tell her to trust her instincts. What I did say, in a momentary pause, was that she shouldn't worry about it and she needed rest.

For Linda, the weeks that followed were painful and frus-trating. For me, they were exhausting and frustrating—but far less than they could have been. I found that it helped to occa-sionally remind myself that during these few weeks I had a unique chance to show Linda a depth of compassion that I wouldn't be able to show her in the months and years ahead. And I had a chance to teach the kids about compassion as well. When the kids and I performed our accident-generated chores, such as helping Linda put on her socks, we assumed the posture of Jesus as he washed the feet of his disciples. It's a healthy posture: a little tough on the back but strengthening to the attitude.

Friends Out of Money

A husband and wife who were good friends of mine came asking for my advice one day, several years ago. People don't do that very often, so I remember it when it happens. The husband had one more semester to go before graduating from the missionary program at a seminary. But they didn't have the money to pay the tuition, and they didn't want to take on any more debt. They had an offer to pastor a church out of state and were thinking about accepting it and finishing seminary later.

What did I think they should do? I understood their problem; I once sat out a quarter of college so I could raise some tuition money. But I worked in a sweltering rubber factory, and there was no chance that I'd get sidetracked and want to make a career of it. I feared that my friends, however, might settle into the pastorate and never finish seminary. So I talked with Linda, and we sent the tuition to the seminary.

Our friends were stunned and a bit embarrassed. They hadn't intended on getting money from me, just advice. But my best advice was for them to finish what they started, especially since they were so close to the end. My wife and I had some extra money in our savings, so the solution seemed obvious. Years later, I was able to visit my friends and their children on the mission field in South America. I was part of a volunteer group helping build a meeting center for regional churches there. Since I edited adult Sunday school curriculum at the time, I was also asked to speak to the local Sunday school teachers. My friend introduced me as an "angel" who had helped his family. But I told the group that before they started thinking of me as an angel, they should consult my mother. Either the joke worked or the translator told them, "He's telling you a joke that you won't get, so just go ahead and laugh."

Shortly after helping our friends, Linda and I decided that it would be a good and godly discipline to regularly set aside money to use when similar needs arise. But we wondered, Where would the money come from? We already tithed on our gross income to the church, and we contributed to charities, though in each case I felt a bit frustrated about throwing money into an impersonal pot without ever knowing how the money was being spent. In fact, out of the approximately $150 billion in total annual charitable contributions in this country—about half of which goes to religious organizations—not even 10 percent goes to "human services," such as direct help for the poor. Most money goes to pay salaries and to build and maintain churches or corporate facilities.

Linda and I decided to begin tithing only on our net income, then using the difference between our net and gross to build a private charity fund. This allows us to continue giving to religious and charitable groups and yet have money available for individuals we come across who need help. Care packages and cash go to a newly divorced lady with young children. Food and toys go to families unemployed at Christmas time. And a new stove goes to an elderly couple whose weary oven has baked its last turkey. Having money already set aside keeps us alert to needs around us that the church and other charitable organizations would miss.

Charities in Search of Support

Charitable organizations go where we can't. They extend the reach of our compassion all the way to Calcutta and beyond, to the ends of the earth. They start in our neighborhoods and work their way out.

In fact, once they started in my family. The summer when my grandmother died and I drove across country to attend her funeral, I had just finished seminary and was engaged to Linda. After I left town, Linda called our pastor to ask the church to pray for my family. The pastor asked if Linda was going to the funeral. She said she couldn't because she wouldn't have the money until payday on Wednesday, the day of the funeral. He told her to come by the church, and he gave her a check for an airline ticket. That may not seem like a big deal to many folks, or even like a wise use of the church's money. But it was a big deal to Linda and me and a graphic reminder of how the church helps people one at a time. Though the money wasn't given as a loan, Linda repaid the gracious gift.

So I've seen how money tossed into impersonal pots can meet personal needs. But I know, too, that we should be careful about where we donate our money. On average, Americans give away about 3 percent of their income. But not all the gifts are wisely given. Some legitimate charities spend nine of every ten dollars on overhead, particularly for salaries, fund-raising, and property.

There are several watchdog organizations to help us discover where our money will make the biggest difference in the lives of individuals. The American Institute of Philanthropy, for example, publishes a quarterly report that dispenses letter grades to several hundred charities. These grades are based on what percentage of the donations is spent on charity (AIP prefers this to be 60 percent or more) and how much it costs each charity to raise $100 (AIP prefers $35 or less).

Well-known charities that drew low grades in a recent report include: Mothers Against Drunk Driving, *D;* Feed the Children/Larry Jones Ministries, *F;* and Shriners Hospital for Crippled Children, whose *A+* was reduced to an *F* because the charity had huge asset reserves of $7.6 billion. "Your dollars are most urgently needed by charities that do not have large reserves of available assets," explained Daniel Borochoff, president of the AIP.

By far, most charities earn *A*'s and *B*'s. Among the many popular charities on the *A* list: American Red Cross, YMCA of the United States, Big Brothers/Big Sisters of America (A+), Cancer Research Institute, and Compassion International.

Overwhelmed by Helplessness

Everywhere we turn there are needs.

Novelist John Grisham, in researching for his book *The Street Lawyer*, left his home in the Virginia countryside to visit the streets and shelters of Washington, D.C. He met young mothers clinging to their children, terrified they would lose their space in the shelter.

He said he cried only once.

It was in a soup kitchen one night when a young mother rushed in with three children, a baby and twin boys about age four, dressed in rags and bone thin. "They attacked a tray of peanut butter sandwiches as if they hadn't seen food in a month," Grisham said. "A volunteer fixed them a plate with cookies, an apple, a cup of vegetable soup, and more sandwiches. They ate furiously, their eyes darting in all directions as if someone might stop them. They stuffed themselves, because they knew the uncertainties of tomorrow."

In North Korea, armed robbers raid private homes for food. Trees in some areas are totally stripped of leaves and edible bark. In some Chinese orphanages that may be spending less than twenty-five cents a day to sustain children, the death rate resembles that of a World War II concentration camp. Shaanxi province's only orphanage took in 232 children in 1989. Nineteen children left that year; 210 died. This death rate compared to new arrivals was about 91 percent—higher than the death rate at Auschwitz, which varied between 70 and 80 percent. The average death rate in Chinese orphanages is an alarming 50 percent.

The sheer magnitude of the problem leaves us dazed. We haven't a clue how we can even begin to make a difference in the world.

I remember my pastor once telling about a little boy strolling along a beach that was covered with starfish that had washed ashore. As the boy walked, he would frequently stoop over, pick up a starfish, and heave it back into the water. An old gent came over to the boy and asked why he bothered, since he couldn't possibly make a difference amid so many stranded starfish. The boy heaved another into the sea and said, "Made a difference to that one."

A seminary ethics professor I know once made the same point another way. He said, "You can't do everything. But you can do something."

My brother Cliff is, among my family, perhaps the most aggressive at helping others. He and his wife run a soup kitchen and clothing pantry that opens its doors one Saturday a month in the fellowship hall of the church he attends. All the workers are volunteers, and most of the food is home-cooked by members of the church. The volunteers serve the people, then fill their own plates and eat alongside them. This is a love feast right out of ancient Christian history, and I can't imagine anything this church does that gives God greater pleasure.

Ted Turner rocked the philanthropic world in 1997 by donating one billion dollars—a third of his wealth—to the United Nations. He said he did it for the cause of world peace. This was the largest monetary gift in history, given by a man who once fired his son by saying, "You're toast."

Some critics attacked Turner, questioning his motives, his reputation for arrogance, and the two billion dollars he kept. But I believe he deserves nothing but sincere thanks. Mother Teresa accepted donations from the former Haitian dictator Jean-Claude "Baby Doc" Duvalier and from savings-and-loan swindler Charles Keating, explaining that the poor would benefit from the gift and the giver would benefit from the giving.

Whether we start a soup kitchen for the hungry and homeless, give a billion dollars for world peace, or buy a stove for an elderly couple, we can all do something. But first we have to change our attitude about money and possessions—a hard task in this brainwashed culture of ours. *Time* magazine in 1997 said Bill Gates was worth more than thirty-six billion dollars. Then the magazine broke this number down to help people grasp its enormity; the editors reported what Gates could buy with all this: a pair of in-line skates for every human being in America or a new Honda Accord LX for every household in his home state of Washington.

An astute reader responded in a letter to the editor.

Aaron Fichtelberg of Chicago wrote, "Your list of 'What Bill Gates Could Buy' did not mention how much food he could buy for the world's hungry, or how much shelter he could provide for the world's homeless. Until America learns wealth is not a measure of virtue, we will always be a poor nation."

CHAPTER 8

A Moment on the Job

It is good and proper for a man ...
to find satisfaction in his toilsome labor under the sun
during the few days of life God has given him.
ECCLESIASTES 5:18

A few months before my boss fired me from my job with an international charity, he assembled the crew of about seventy-five workers and gave us a short motivational talking-to.

Actually, he gave good advice: "You spend about a third of your time in bed and a third of your time at work. So make sure you have a comfortable mattress and a good job."

This was a warning. He knew that some of us were uncomfortable with a recent decision he had made to hire a fund-raising company that specialized in writing exaggerated appeal letters to donors. (The more urgent the request for help, this company argued, the more money you get to do good deeds.) I believe that in his speech the boss was telling each one of his employees to plant both feet firmly on board his ship or take a flying leap. One middle manager leapt quickly. Three others of us—a newly hired grant writer from Washington, D.C.; a director of donor contributions; and me, the editorial director—apparently didn't act quickly enough to suit him; he fired us all on the same day, shortly before Christmas and only three months after my wife and I had bought our first house.

The president told me I could stay until the end of the year, but after he saw me joyously singing Christmas carols with others at the company Christmas party, he politely told me to leave by week's end and to take my severance pay with me. He realized, correctly, that it was demoralizing to other frustrated employees to see me so happy after being fired. It made them feel as if they could get happy, too, if they left.

I had taken the job a year earlier, excited about working for the charity to which my coal miner grandfather had regularly contributed, decades earlier. They did wonderful work, and still do, but they became dishonest in their fund-raising appeals. An old hospital boiler in need of replacement, for instance, got written up in a fund-raising letter as a boiler about to blow.

For a time, some of us thought we could change the organization's strategy. We believed that we could convince the president and the board of directors that, though exaggeration and deception might bring in more money in the short run, over the long haul contributors would eventually discover what was going on, and with their pocketbooks they would cast their vote of opposition.

That was almost twenty years ago. Just recently the news broke that this organization was among a small handful of child sponsorship charities that didn't always use sponsorship money in ways that directly benefited the children. Instead, according to news reports, some of the money went to community services.

In looking back on all of this, I'm glad I got fired. Though I had already started searching for other work, without the firing I might have lingered in that distressing job for months. Maybe years. A colleague who seemed as upset as I was about the goings-on is still there, explaining that the salary is too good to leave.

An ancient Hebrew poem comes to mind: "Each man's life is but a breath.... He bustles about, but only in vain; he heaps up wealth, not knowing who will get it" (Psalm 39:5-6). When I come to the end of my career—which will be in a moment, as the Spirit measures time—I'll want to see more than plump IRAs, mutual funds, and cash reserve accounts. As Jesus once advised a man bickering with a brother over the family inheritance, "A man's life does not consist in the abundance of his possessions" (Luke 12:15). When I look over my shoulder at the career I leave behind, I'll want to see recollections of a job that was worth doing well.

Unhappy Working Stiffs

Recent surveys in the workplace show that, when people come to the end of their career, many have no intention of looking back. They'll want nothing but distance between them and their former job.

Nearly three out of four working people said they wish they had explored more career options, according to a Gallup survey conducted for the National Career Development Association. In another study, of 693 people throughout the country, almost half said they would have chosen a different career if they knew then what they know now.

Why do so many folks end up in the wrong line of work? Two reasons stand out. First, many people fall into a job without any serious thought or plan, reported the Gallup poll. Only about one in three said they carefully chose their career. Others took what was available at the time, acting on tips from friends, ads in the media, or cold calls made throughout the community.

That's how I got my first job during high school. Dad, who's a great mechanic, got me a job at a gas station back when workers pumped gas, cleaned windows, checked under the hood, and repaired cars in the garage bay. During college, an acquaintance of my mom got me a higher-paying job in a rubber factory, where he worked as a foreman.

Second, many build career strategies on shifting sand. These job hunters choose their careers based on what they excelled at in school or in aptitude tests. So says a twelve-year study in which Harvard Business School tracked the careers of more than 650 business professionals. People can excel in math and science, for example, and not enjoy either. Skills and the demand for those skills shift over time, but a person's deepest interests generally remain bedrock stable from early adulthood on.

Career counselors—in a rapidly growing specialty spawned of changes caused by technology and by the fact that developing countries now make products they used to buy from America—urge job hunters to start their search by looking within and discovering their interests and values.

By the time I was in high school, I enjoyed writing and did well in writing classes. Teachers suggested I consider a career in writing, an idea I initially resisted. I was born in the fifties, when if you asked your dad how the day went he'd say, "Every day's hard when you're trying to make a living." Nearly every-one I knew worked at physically demanding, dangerous jobs in factories and coal mines. I found it difficult to grab hold of the idea that I could make a living in an air-conditioned office, doing something I loved.

Values are another important matter for job hunters. For example, if you're driven by a sense of service and you want to leave the world a better place, forget becoming a spin doctor for politicians. Instead, consider medicine, counseling, or ministry. And if you value security more than the freedom to try creative ideas, don't launch your own business. Head for a workplace less prone to change, like a large corporation or the federal government.

Here are a few other value issues to consider, if you hope to feel happy and fulfilled in your job: Do you want to be the best you can possibly be in your field? Are praise and recognition important to you? Do you want the big bucks (regardless of Jesus' many warnings about wealth, and the fact that he who dies with the most toys . . . dies)? If you can name your values, you can make better choices.

"Values are rudders in life," says Linda Leahy, a career consultant and co-owner of Career Success Services in Des Plaines, Illinois. "They determine where we want to go and get us there." Leahy adds that "everyone has an inner voice that informs us what is important. Many of the job problems our clients have can be traced to their not paying attention to that voice."

When it comes to listening to my inner voice, I've been a slow learner and a skeptic who needs convincing. In my last job before becoming a freelance writer and editor, I worked as a magazine and book editor for a denominational headquarters. I produced a magazine about life in Bible times and a line of books and accompanying leader's guides about modern religious issues; both products were used in adult Sunday school classes in a coalition of denominations that had similar beliefs.

I wanted not only to produce the best products on the market, anywhere in the country, but also to be the "can-do" guy in the office. Whatever my supervisors asked of me, I wanted to say, "Sure, I can do that." Within a few years my work load increased dramatically. Of course.

I was writing on assignment for other editors in the organization. I was asked to design and produce a one-year curriculum package for newcomers to the church—a type of catechism. I led workshops throughout the country. And all the while, I continued editing my original products, which had been a full-time job. I loved my work, but there was far more of it than I could handle.

About the time I fell one year behind in my deadlines, an editor managed to transfer one of his smaller editing projects to my desk. That was the death of the "can-do" guy. I went to my supervisor and gently protested by using what is now a politically incorrect visual image: "I feel like I've been carrying a fat lady on my back, and somebody just tossed her an apple."

My boss smiled and admitted that I was carrying more than my share of the work load. But he asked that I try it for a while and see how it went. My part-time editorial assistant soon began working with me nearly full time, and she took on many of the editorial tasks I had been doing. Eventually, we finished the newcomer's curriculum, I dropped the seminars, and I caught up with my deadlines. But all of these happened only because I learned to start saying, "No."

As a result, I enjoyed my job more.

I made the switch from "can-do" to "no way" not only because of the stresses I experienced but because of the wise advice of a colleague. He told me that the honchos of the system—any system—will work you to death if you let them. He said they'll come to your funeral, lay flowers on your grave, then they'll look up and say, "Next?"

I wish I had known, when I first took that job, what was only recently discovered in a study conducted by the University of California and Stanford University. Perhaps I would have backed away from the overload much earlier, after reading that the happiest people focus on their own values rather than compare their performance to others.

The study involved fifty undergraduate students who had scored either high or low on happiness tests. Each student was asked to solve a set of word puzzles and was tested alongside another student in cahoots with the researchers. The accomplices had been told to fake their answers and quickly breeze through the test. Happy and unhappy students scored equally well, but the students prone to unhappiness expressed greater doubts about their work.

The conclusion? Social psychologist Sonja Lyubomirsky said that the world is full of people who seem to be doing better than we are: they're smarter, richer, better looking. But we should resist the temptation to compare ourselves to them. "Happy people pay attention to their own internal standards," Lyubomirsky said, "so it matters less to them how everybody else is doing."

When It's Time to Leave

As is the case with many denominational publishers, my publication budgets were small. As a result, quality was not Job One. Thrift was Job One. But quality was an important value to me. I wanted everything I wrote or edited to be the best I could produce. But in that job setting, with tiny budgets and with bosses and coworkers who were trained as pastors instead of editors, I was forever swimming upstream with ideas for improving my products.

When I pressed for more photos in a text-heavy magazine, none of my colleagues saw the value of photos, just the extra expense and research the photos would require. Yet they graciously agreed to let me present my case to the production committee. There, I not only had to debate the production manager (that's a given, for editors), I actually had to go nose-to-nose with the art director. He didn't want any photos at all. An art director who didn't want art. Go figure.

Surprisingly, the picture idea got a green light anyhow. I don't know if this was because the production committee realized that we live in a visual age or because they got weary of listening to me talk and they wanted to go to lunch. Perhaps all of the above.

As it turned out, the picture idea worked out well. Magazine subscriptions grew, and we eventually received the Evangelical Press Association's Award of Excellence, akin to the Oscar in evangelical magazine publishing. Even the art director was happy.

In spite of the occasional frustrations, I loved the work. My favorite part was getting to ask the best biblical scholars in my theological tradition some of the hardest questions about the

Bible. Then I'd publish their answers in articles and commentaries used in adult Sunday school classes.

Curriculum runs in cycles, though. And after about a dozen years in this assignment, I started getting restless and began thinking about other jobs. Two events prodded me to do more than think. First, my supervisor, who had graciously held the reigns loosely over me, announced he was retiring. Second, our denominational leaders began making plans to restructure the entire operation of the headquarters.

I smelled trouble.

Career counselors give quizzes to help people know when it's time to find a new job. Answering yes to most of the following questions—variations of which are commonly used by counselors—is a clue to hit the road running.

1. Are continuing education opportunities withering and your job skills getting stale?

2. Are you and your boss clashing more often or with stronger emotions?

3. Is the freedom you have to do your job being eroded by bureaucratic obstacles or control-minded supervisors?

4. Is your company having money troubles?

5. Are big changes ahead, such as administrative reorganization?

6. Have you hit a dead-end in your salary or your job advancement opportunities?

7. Are you out of the loop, and among the last to hear about important decisions affecting you?

8. Do you hate going to work?

9. Is company morale lower than dirt?

10. Are the brightest and best people leaving?

If you answer yes to several of these questions, you should think about putting out feelers for a new job. If you answer yes to most of the questions, as I did, you don't need to think about anything. You need a new job. The sooner, the better.

As I considered job options, only one idea sparked my interest. I wanted to stay in my field of Christian journalism, but I couldn't get excited about remaining with the headquarters or moving into another corporate setting. Having worked so long in a restrictive assignment limited by budgets and phobias of new ideas, I felt like a butterfly trapped in a cocoon. I wanted to spread my wings and fly. I wanted to try freelance writing and editing full time. In fact, I had already been testing the wind by the light of the moon and had developed a good working relationship with some national publishing companies.

A friend of mine who was a book editor, however, offered his sobering observation. He said the best thing about freelancing is that it lets you pick where you'll starve. He wasn't the only person worried about me. On the January morning when I walked into my retiring supervisor's office, closed his door, and told him of my plans, he veiled his concern within a compliment: "I know you won't do anything to jeopardize your family."

His fear, of course, was that this is exactly what I was doing. Clearly, he knew the risks of freelancing. And I appreciated both his tact and his worry. He spoke of the security that headquarters employees have: this organization weathered the Great Depression, and rarely was anyone fired.

Yet for me, the risk of staying seemed greater than the risk of leaving. If I stayed, I might become a disagreeable old editor with the stomach lining of a soap bubble. Or worse, if I stopped bucking the status quo and gave up pitching new ideas, I might become just another unfulfilled editor sleepwalking through the motions of a job I no longer enjoyed.

On the other hand, if I left, I could pursue one of life's greatest joys: "A man can do nothing better than to eat and drink and find satisfaction in his work" (Ecclesiastes 2:24). Since life is but a moment, experienced in a breath, I took a calculated leap.

The decision was more of a no-brainer than my worried friends realized. Financially, my family would be better off—even if I earned nothing. Linda had been working only part time as a nurse. But working full time, she would bring home more than the two of us had been earning together. And our time would be more flexible. Full time for her required only an average of three twelve-hour shifts a week. And her workdays would be clustered in such a way that she would have about a week off each month.

Many weeks before announcing my resignation, I met with our accountant to get her advice. Then I called my top freelance clients to let them know when I would be available full time. I also talked with Linda's dad, to get his blessing—much as I had done earlier, before proposing marriage. He's from the generation in which men did "men" things and women stayed home. I didn't want him to think that I was going to dump the weight of the family finances on Linda while I relaxed with daytime soap operas. He blessed me.

Happy Working Stiffs

Life is too short to waste in unfulfilling jobs.

I know we have to feed our families. But especially in a country with the widely varied opportunities that we have, we shouldn't settle for jobs we dread going to each day. I also know that God calls some of us to take on tough assignments.

The ten most stressful jobs in America, according to the American Institute of Stress, are these:

- Inner-city high school teacher
- Police officer
- Miner
- Air traffic controller
- Medical intern
- Stockbroker
- Journalist
- Customer service/complaint worker
- Waiter
- Secretary

All these groups fit the profile of high-stress jobs: unrelenting demands, a work load controlled by others, the need to constantly stay alert, the prospect of drastic consequences if mistakes are made, and the side effect of work spilling into leisure time. Yet we need all these people, even stockbrokers, who are protecting and nurturing our college and retirement funds.

I believe that God gives people the interests, values, and skills to do the job before them, or he gives an inner voice that whispers, "Pick a direction and run away as fast as you can." There's an increasing number of compasses to help us choose a wise direction: toll-free phone lines identifying local career counselors, such as those recommended by the National Board for Certified Counselors; hundreds of tests that measure interests, values, and aptitude; Web sites with career resources and job listings; and books such as the annually updated *What Color Is Your Parachute?* with advice about rethinking careers, changing jobs, and finding counselors.

Once we find the right job—and surveys say that about half of us already have—we can experience for ourselves what the sage of Ecclesiastes discovered only after analyzing all he had seen of life. Perhaps spurred on by a mid-life crisis, or an eyeball-to-dustball encounter with his own mortality, he started thinking about why humans exist. At first, he saw no point to life or to the work that occupies so much of our time: "Utterly meaningless! Everything is meaningless. What does man gain from all his labor at which he toils under the sun? Generations come and generations go, but the earth remains forever" (1:3-4). No matter what we do, the sage explained, the sun rises and sets in a cycle that we are powerless to disturb. The wind blows where it pleases. And rivers return to the sea. We humans make no difference.

Fortunately, that wasn't his last word.

Life, he concluded, is a mysterious gift from God. We can't understand it. But we can and should enjoy it. So, in the words of my ex-boss, "make sure you have a comfortable mattress and a good job."

CHAPTER 9

The Moment
of Retirement

I have come that they may have life,
and have it to the full.
JOHN 10:10

I don't have to leave my immediate family to get two radi-
cally clashing opinions about retirement.

"It stinks," says my mom. She retired last year, at age sixty-
three, from teaching elementary school.

For the opposing view, there's my father-in-law, Donald
Burnes, seventy-two: "Retirement can be the most fun time of
your life." He should know. He has retired so often that you
have to plot a timeline to count them: from the Air Force in
1974, from pastoring an American servicemen's church in
Japan in 1984, from pastoring a servicemen's church in
Germany in 1990, from speaking as an evangelist in 1992, then
from a year of interim pastoring in Oklahoma in 1995.
Someday, perhaps, he'll retire from his current part-time job as
chaplain for several retirement homes.

I know. It sounds like my father-in-law's in denial. If retirement's so great, why does he keep taking new jobs? Because
he can. That's what retirement is, as far as he's concerned.
"I'm doing what I want to, when I want to," he explains, "and

I don't have to worry about a paycheck and having enough to eat."

My mom has plenty to eat too. In fact, she tells me that she's gained ten pounds since retiring. That's because she's been passing her time by baking. Cream puffs. Pies. Cookies. Cakes. Bread from scratch. You name it, she'll bake it. She retired early to spend more time with Dad, who in recent years has been struggling through chemotherapy treatments for cancer. But Dad's been doing well lately and has returned to his hobbies of woodworking and repairing the aging cars, appliances, and engine-powered toys of his children and tribe of grandchildren living nearby.

"It's an adjustment," Mom says of her retirement. "You lose your old friends. People don't call. You don't feel you fit in anywhere, so you work your fanny off trying to find things to do—to find your niche."

Mom has taken to exercising a couple times a week at an indoor pool. Sometimes, a busload of school children will arrive on a fun outing, and she'll mosey over to them, striking up a conversation here and there. Back at home, a four-year-old neighbor girl stops by once in awhile to chat. Hope is her name. She came over a few days before my latest visit to Mom and Dad's. Hope said she needed money for her savings account. Mom said she did, too, and wondered if Hope knew where they could get any. (Tell me Mom doesn't know how to handle kids.)

Hope then tried a different approach, announcing that her birthday was coming soon and that she'd like Mom to get her something. Mom replied that she just had a birthday herself and nobody got her anything.

That's when Hope unloaded an innocent zinger: "If you

get me something for my birthday, I'll get you something if you have another birthday." If? Was this a hiccup in speech or the insight of a miniature prophet?

"I think retirement is synonymous with death," ninety-year-old Arthur Goodfriend recently told *Time* magazine. A former Army lieutenant colonel, Goodfriend became the oldest person to serve in the Peace Corps when he taught English in Hungary during the early 1990s. He recently completed his second tour as a VISTA volunteer.

My father-in-law would agree with Goodfriend, for very personal reasons. "Dad was a rancher," Don says. "He was riding horses when he was seventy-five years old. And they weren't slow horses."

But Don's brother, who had taken over running the ranch, was afraid for their dad. The elderly rancher usually stayed at his son's home on the lower part of the land, outside Forsyth, Montana. But sometimes he stayed in the house at the upper ranch. Alone there, he could take a fall. And with the snow-blinding blizzards of winter coming, he could die before anyone would get to him.

It was agreed he should retire completely from ranching and move to town. He stayed in the old Joseph Hotel, converted into a retirement center. For the next three-and-a-half months he spent most of his waking hours sitting by a window in the lobby, looking outside. Sometimes he played checkers. Sometimes he took a walk. But for a man used to working hard for sixteen hours a day, being put out to pasture like an aging horse cut from the herd was more than he could handle. On a frigid January morning he climbed the flight of stairs to his room, and he lay down on his bed to nap. He never got up. When he failed to show up for lunch, he was discovered dead of heart failure. For the three days that Don spent in town for his dad's funeral, the temperature stuck at twenty-two degrees below zero. Montana blizzards can kill, but so can boredom. No one knows if the old rancher would have lived longer on his own land, doing what chores he could handle. But everyone wonders.

The final moment God gives us on this planet—the time of our retirement—shouldn't be spent apart from our loved ones, staring hours on end out a hotel window (or into a mind-draining TV). Experts on aging agree that, inasmuch as it's within our power, our moment of retirement should be one of continuing adventure, ever-increasing fulfillment, and a joyful lust for life. As the writer of Ecclesiastes curtly put it, "You may live a long time and have a hundred children. But a child born dead is better off than you, unless you enjoy life" (6:3, *Contemporary English Version*).

How to Savor Retirement

Here are a few suggestions from older adults looking over their shoulders at scenes from the past. They share blunders they made in retirement planning and living, as well as successes.

Develop a Money Plan
Then run with it. When my father-in-law was in the Air Force, his family of six lived from one paycheck to the next. He did manage to sock away a little retirement money into bonds, but he quickly used it all when his oldest child started college. Fortunately, he recovered enough to enjoy what has become a

modest but pleasant retirement with the help of a couple pensions, Social Security, rental income from one of his former homes, and part-time work.

Saving little or nothing for retirement is perilously common. One in three people has not saved a red cent, according to a study of one thousand adults, conducted for the Employee Benefit Retirement Institute and the American Savings Education Council. Nearly nine of ten say they aren't saving enough.

With those kinds of numbers, it's not surprising that one in four of the nearly 250 retirees in the study said they never even bothered to estimate how much they would need for retirement. Frankly, I understand that cynical sense of "why bother?" How can anyone predict the amount of money we'll need for retirement? We haven't a clue what's going to happen to the value of our money once we leave the job force and start living off our fixed investments. We don't know what kind of health-care expenses we'll face. And we have no idea how long we'll live.

Yet even as I spout skepticism, my family's entire financial history is in a box somewhere in the office of a carefully selected financial planner. We're asking for advice about saving for retirement and for the college education of our two kids. We've been saving for many years, investing in mutual funds, bonds, and certificates of deposit. But we want an expert evaluation of what we've done so far and of what we should try to do in the years ahead.

We expect that our planner will tell us to do a better job of balancing risky investments with the more conservative. Since we're still about twenty years from retirement, we've probably erred on the side of risk. So far, the strategy has paid off well, often providing more than 15 percent interest each year. But this can't last. If it could, the stock market wouldn't be the stock market; it would be a free lunch.

Though financial planners, retirement kits, and fiscal formulas aren't infallible—and are constantly being adjusted as our economy and standard of living change—they can give us ballpark numbers to monitor our progress into and through retirement. In so doing, they help send us on our way into tomorrow with our eyes wide open and our nest egg tucked safely away.

A word about retirement doomsayers, those survey-packin' suits who paralyze us with scenes of working till we're seventy-five and then dining on dog food. There are two points they generally fail to mention.

First, they don't volunteer that their salaries come from investment companies that stand to cash in big time on a retirement panic, or from megacorporations only too happy to back away from company-funded pensions in favor of programs paid for primarily, or exclusively, by the workers.

Second, they choose not to mention that retirees are spared from many expenses of years past. Peak spending years are between ages forty-five and fifty-four, reports the Bureau of Labor Statistics. After that, expenses ratchet down as we live more simply and cheaply. Our house payments become a matter of history; or, better yet, we've traded down for a house that's smaller and more manageable. We probably don't need two vehicles, and the one we keep won't be driven to work every day. We can skip the business apparel. And we get to enjoy our reduced tax rates and our great senior-citizen discounts.

Don't Retire to a Recliner

During the century before Christ, the Roman philosopher Lucretius once asked, "Why doest thou not retire like a guest sated [filled] with the banquet of life, and with calm mind embrace, thou fool, a rest that knows no care?"

Lucretius must not have visited many retirement homes. There, folks who do as Lucretius advises are among the most pitied. Retirement centers where my father-in-law ministers are hives of busyness: people leaving for the movies, returning from the Great Mall of the Great Plains, loading into a van to try out a new Asian restaurant. Some people are power-walking the inside corridor square, where eight laps is a mile. But the pitied watch TV, eat a meal, then return to the TV until the next mealtime. That's a "rest that knows no care." So's a coma.

There are two kinds of retirement. There's the comatose rest that knows no care. That's the kind of retirement that former Army lieutenant colonel Goodfriend says is "synonymous with death." And there's doing what you want, when you want.

That's the kind of retirement practiced by Sister Gertrude Ann Theisen of Rochester, Minnesota. Though seventy-three years old, crippled by arthritis, and forced to get around in an Amigo (a three-wheeled, battery-powered wheelchair), she made a pilgrimage to a church in Lourdes, France. The church was built to commemorate what many believe was an 1858 visit by the Virgin Mary; people make pilgrimages there for healing of body and spirit. There, outside the church, a police-man pulled the nun over for speeding.

Sister Gertrude Ann was driving her wheelchair at the time. It doesn't go more than five miles per hour.

She explained to me that the church service had just been dismissed, and everyone was rushing through a pelting rain to get back to their hotels. Sister Gertrude Ann's hotel was a half-mile away, and in front of her rolled a slow-moving line of perhaps twenty wheelchairs. Worried that her three-wheeler might short out in the rain, she pulled onto the road to pass the four-wheelers.

That's when a *gendarme* raised his arm and took out his ticket pad. Apparently, wheelchairs are supposed to hold their position, a bit like Formula One race cars under a yellow flag. A French-speaking woman in Sister Gertrude Ann's group talked to the policeman, perhaps asking if he was really going to give a ticket to an elderly nun in a wheelchair. The policeman cracked a smile and waved the pilgrims on.

Sister Gertrude Ann is now seventy-eight. She's had knee and hip replacements. She wears braces on both knees, her neck, and her back. But she works part-time as a librarian at the Southeastern Minnesota Center for Independent Living. She dresses up as Dottie the Clown to entertain and teach arthritis patients how to take care of themselves. And, driving her Amigo, she boards a lift-equipped bus that takes her to the mall, where she cruises the shops.

For those of us who want to stay alive and enjoy a long retirement, there's compelling evidence for following in the wheelchair tracks of Sister Gertrude Ann or in the footsteps of retired soldier Goodfriend and my father-in-law. A growing body of research suggests that most incapacitating illnesses are not an inevitable consequence of aging, as many have believed, but are more often the result of lifestyle choices we make about exercise, food, relationships, and mental stimulation.

Aerobic exercise, the kind that my father-in-law gets on fast-paced daily walks, feeds life-preserving oxygen to heart, lungs, and brain, helping keep the tissues alive. Tissues not only weaken from disuse; some of it dies and won't regenerate. A diet based on low-fat food that is rich in nutrients not only prevents heart disease, the Western world's leading cause of early death, but it can reverse some of the damage. So reveals a study by San Francisco cardiologist Dean Ornish.

Other studies show that high blood pressure is not part of the natural aging process, though it affects one third of Americans in their fifties, half of those in their sixties, and more than two-thirds of those over seventy. It's the result of eating processed food, teeming with tissue-absorbing salt and artery-clogging fat. Dr. Paul Whelton of Tulane University's School of Public Health has spent the past decade tracking fifteen thousand rural farmers in southwestern China. As long as they eat their traditional food—a little meat along with a lot of rice, vegetables, and fruit—they don't develop high blood pressure. But when they move to town, their blood pressures rise with age. "Their genes don't change when they move," Whelton explained. "Their diet does."

Maintaining a network of family and friends, rather than a network of favorite television programs, does far more than merely enrich our lives. It extends our lives. One study of elderly heart-attack patients showed that those who had two or more close friends were twice as likely to survive the first year than were the friendless.

Mental workouts are critical for memory and overall brain function. Unlike tissue cells elsewhere in our body, the billions of brain neurons (nerve cells) that send commands via electrical signals to neighboring neurons don't divide. When they weaken through lack of use and later die, connections are forever broken. Other neurons, however, may be able to establish new connections through what amounts to a detour. If these new pathways are used often enough, the bond grows stronger; so does memory, as well as other functions of the brain. The standing prescription regarding the brain is one that echoes the adage we hear in fitness centers: Use it or lose it. Exercise the brain by reading, going to art museums, working puzzles, discussing current issues, or taking on a new field of study, anything from bird-watching to accounting to a foreign language.

What's the alternative to retirement in a recliner? Billy Graham, eighty, is fighting Parkinson's disease, a progressive nerve disorder that has sapped his strength, forced him to cut back in his ministry, and made it impossible for him to drive or to write by hand. But he politely rebuffs any queries about retiring: "The New Testament says nothing of apostles who retired and took it easy."

Argus Tresidder, ninety-one, calls this decade of his life the "no-no period." No fatty food, no salt, no alcohol, no sex, and very little eyesight. Problems with glaucoma, cataracts, and a detached retina have left him legally blind. Yet no part of his day is idle. He rises at 7 A.M. to a light breakfast, left in the fridge by one of his volunteer caretakers the night before. A walking companion arrives afterward, and they head for the rugged park nearby or the basement treadmill if the weather's bad. That's his favorite time of the day because he enjoys the talk that accompanies the walk. "Companionship is the spice of life for the elderly," he says.

After a shower, he writes for the rest of the morning. He has written novels, children's stories, and plays, which are proofread by volunteers. Although he has published six books and many articles, he has faced years of disappointing rejection by publishers. Yet he hopes someone will discover him as a writer, even posthumously. In the meantime, he says it's fun to keep trying.

After lunch with his caretaker he spends the afternoon listening to Library of Congress Talking Books and keeping up with the news through radio and recorded magazines. Three evenings a week, people come to read to him. He goes to parties, flies to visit friends in other cities, and is considering attending the seventieth reunion of his college class.

Merle McEathron, 102, knows all about accepting losses, yet she's no quitter. When she was just seven, she found her mother dead of a heart attack on the floor of the family home in Vincennes, Indiana. As the oldest girl, Merle took over many of her mother's chores in caring for her little sister, her two older brothers, and her dad. She remembers standing on a box so she could reach the stove to cook.

She married at fifteen, but her husband left her ten years later, with two sons to care for. She started a general store and put both boys through college. During World War II she worked as a housemother at the Cadet Club, a military social center for young airmen, who took her for rides in fighter planes.

She was fifty-one when the war ended and she moved to Phoenix. After outliving her second and third husbands, she moved herself into the Eastern Star retirement center. Then at age ninety-eight, she broke a leg. The doctor said she'd never walk again. But she got herself a walker, clunked her way to the exercise room, and got busy working on the injured limb. She worked it hard enough that she was eventually able to get around with a cane. Then she worked the leg some more and threw away the cane. At age 102 she walks a mile and a quarter each day. Every September, she travels to Indiana for the Cadet Club reunion, where she climbs up the wing of a restored World War II training plane, buckles herself into the cockpit behind the pilot, and rides into the blue.

Volunteer, travel, or take a temporary job. All of these avenues are opening wide for retirees. My mom, not content with baking and then swimming off the calories and the creaks, is looking into volunteering her time at a children's hospital; she's even considering a stint in the Peace Corps.

My father-in-law and his wife love to travel, a pastime that seems bred into military families. Lately, he has been praising Elderhostel, a Boston-based, nonprofit network of educational and service programs throughout all fifty of the United States and more than seventy countries. Voyagers aged fifty-five and older can, for instance, explore volcanoes in Hawaii, study literature in New England, or conduct field research in Belize to save the dolphins. Only 220 people participated in 1975. This year, some three hundred thousand will take part in one of more than ten thousand programs.

Temporary work is attracting retirees around the country, says Bruce Steinberg, research director at the National Association of Temporary and Staffing Services. In the latest survey of their sixteen hundred member companies, more than one of ten workers were retirees. "People are living longer and need money to fill financial gaps of Social Security," Steinberg told a reporter for the *Chicago Tribune*. "But most of our retirees do temp work to be busy and have contact with other people." Employers are especially receptive to hiring older workers because they tend to be experienced, industrious, and dependable. An added bonus is their upbeat attitude and the friendly way they treat customers and coworkers.

Think Twice Before Moving

Most retirees stay where they've sunk their roots. That keeps them near family and longtime friends and in familiar surroundings. But about 10 percent pull up roots and replant themselves, usually in a milder climate. That percentage may rise as the seventy-five million well-traveled baby boomers start retiring soon. Born between 1946 and 1964, the boomers are turning fifty. Many are headed for early retirement.

It's a mistake, say experts, to choose a retirement location on the basis of happy vacations. One recently retired couple, like many, decided to get away from cold winters. They chose Myrtle Beach, South Carolina, a place they had fallen in love with during two vacations. In the autumn, they bought a home with a shoreline view. But in May, when vacationers invaded the beach community, traffic became a perpetual rush hour. The beaches, golf courses, and restaurants they had enjoyed churned into a tangle of humanity. The couple moved again, inland enough to get away from the crush, yet within a short drive of Myrtle Beach's attractions, which they seized upon during the off-season.

In a survey of subscribers to *Where to Retire* magazine, one big mistake that the readers own up to is that they should have rented a year before buying. Experts agree that, if you're going to uproot yourself to a new region, you should first spend some year-round time there.

Still, there are situations that call for an out-of-state move. My wife's parents expected to live out their years in Altus, Oklahoma, near the Air Force base from which my father-in-law retired. Though the closest relative was several hundred miles away, Linda's parents had plenty of friends in the area. They had the luxury of base facilities, such as free health care, a free fitness center, and subsidized groceries from the commissary. But when Don needed open-heart surgery, followed two years later by gall bladder surgery, his wife each time found herself all but stranded. She doesn't drive, and the small town didn't have a convenient transportation program. Some of the kids, Linda included, converged on the home to help their mom and dad.

As Don began to heal from the second surgery, he and his wife made the hard decision to move. But where? They wanted to be near one of their four children, scattered amid Texas, Colorado, Kansas, and Missouri, but any of these families might have to pull up stakes and follow the job market to a new town. They decided to move seven-tenths of a mile from us (I measured the distance).

That put them within a two-hour drive of their Kansas daughter and within a ten-minute walk of us. Linda is a registered nurse, so they may have figured, correctly, that she would become an advocate for them in their health care, explaining matters that doctors sometimes rush through. Since I work as a freelance writer for publishers throughout the country, they probably guessed that we would be the least likely to move.

I had always gotten along well with them, but I was a bit nervous. I've seen tensions erupt among family members living close together, and I wondered if this would happen to us. I also worried a tad about how to strike a balance between raising our incredibly active kids and helping out the grandparents.

As it turns out, the grandparents should have been worrying about how they could maintain their busy schedule in church, ministry in the retirement homes, volunteering in community programs, and attending to the needs of my family. The grinding cycle of our kids' piano recitals, baseball games, soccer games, basketball games, along with school and youth group fund-raisers—to name just a few—would leave many grandparents praying, "Thy kingdom come." But Linda's folks are there for Rebecca and Bradley.

They've been there for Linda and me too. When Linda fell at work, her mom prepared our supper for weeks, and her dad drove Linda to doctors' appointments and physical therapy as I grappled with deadlines and, in my off-hours, rushed about to perform all the chores that Linda and I had previously shared.

Actually, we're honing this seven-tenths of a mile lifestyle into an art form of mutual support. We cut their grass, help out with home improvement projects, and haul pickup-truck loads of big goodies coming in or yard waste going out. They help us by giving a landing place or a ride for the kids, watching our home when we're out of town, and inviting us over for impromptu, fast-paced suppers when they know we're rushed.

Getting to Know Your Family

There's one other benefit of retirement that I'd like to mention, and it has to do with Linda's parents living so close to us. I understand this particular issue best from the perspective of a son-in-law.

Because Linda works twelve-hour shifts, usually clustered

three days at a time, her time at home comes in clumps too. For example, once a month she has eight consecutive days off work. It's not unusual at all for her to spend one or more of those days with her parents, running errands, shopping for who knows what, and trying out new restaurants at lunchtime.

The benefit I'm talking about is illustrated in one of my January journal entries:

Linda is off work today. She took her mom to the doctor this morning, leaving here at 8:30, while her dad ran a college kid to the airport [part of their community volunteering]. I prophesied that Linda would be gone all day. She said not. She called at 11:30 and said she was going to grab a sandwich at a nearby Subway and asked if I wanted to join them. I asked them to bring it home and eat with me, which they did. They had "stopped at the store" after the doctor visit, which is why they were so late.

After lunch I thought Linda would work through the laundry mountain obscuring the hamper at the end of our upstairs hall. Not today. She took her mom home two hours ago, and I haven't heard from her since.

But I'm not angry. Honest. I'm thinking of a scene from the Bible. Jesus is visiting with Mary and Martha. Martha is busy doing housework, while Mary is with Jesus—while she still has time. Jesus will be gone too soon.

Linda will always have housework. She'll not always have her mom.

I know there's a balance to be found there, but if the scales are going to be tipped a little offside—and they generally are—they should be tipped on the side of spending time with her folks.

Linda is doing now what she was not able to do as a child: develop and nurture an intimate bond with her parents. As a military kid, Linda saw her dad far too little; he was so often away on temporary duty assignments or in Vietnam. Also hard to come by was closeness with her mom, who lived in ceaseless stress over trying to manage a family of six on a serviceman's pay, along with hassling over the constant moves to different bases—some of which were overseas, requiring Don to go ahead and the family to follow six to nine months later.

But here, in retirement, endearing bonds are being forged. There is laughing. At times there is crying, as when grandfather baptizes granddaughter. On occasion there is grandmotherly trickery at board games, followed by youthful accusations and entertaining denials.

Retirement, as it turns out, can be a time to do life's most important work, which in years gone by was bumped aside in the frantic effort to survive.

CHAPTER 10

The Moment of Death

The length of our days is seventy years—or eighty,
if we have the strength.... They quickly pass, and we fly away.
PSALM 90:10

The announcement was made during our Sunday school class. If any of us wanted to see our classmate Ron before he died, we should go to the hospital that week.

Ron was a forty-five-year-old dentist, newly divorced, and the father of two teenagers. Friendly and often joking, he had stood long and lanky sipping coffee and feasting on donuts during our class's social time. He wore a thin and drawn hound-dog face, which he tried to fill out with a gray beard. But that only made his face look longer, though comfortably approachable.

I didn't know Ron well. Just snippets from our short, lively exchanges: while married, he had loved showering with his gorgeous wife, he knew how to do the Dance of the Red Tape with managed health-care bureaucrats, and he chose to take his brain cancer chemotherapy while on vacation in the Caribbean. "If you have to get chemo," he said, "why not get it near a beach?"

I almost decided against making the forty-five-minute drive

to North Kansas City Hospital. Ron was not a close friend. And I was busy, working toward another project deadline. But in the early afternoon of Monday, I felt strangely compelled to stop what I was doing and go see him. Linda was off work that day, so we went together.

On the door of Ron's private room hung a handwritten sign: "Stop and see the nurse." That sounds ominous, I thought. Linda and I walked to the nurses' station, just a few steps away, and said we were there to see Ron. The nurse asked if we were family.

"We're from his Sunday school class," I said. That must have carried some weight for her. She immediately let us in, warning that Ron would probably fall asleep soon because he had just gotten back from his daily radiation treatment and had been given some strong medication for pain.

Ron's hair lay long and wavy on the pillow. His graying beard seemed a bit long too and in need of a trim. Ron was thinner than I remembered from our class's Stockton Lake swim party; his skin looked shrink-wrapped over his rib cage. Into the core of his chest ran a central IV line, which health-care workers use when veins are in danger of collapse.

Even so, Ron's pose seemed relaxed, even ... Caribbean. He lay in bed with his left leg resting on his propped up right knee, as though he were lounging on the beach. His skin was still beautifully bronzed from his chemo-by-the-sea vacation. I remember thinking, *He's going to die with a tan.*

When Ron heard our footsteps, he opened his right eye and spoke in whispers. "Hi, guy."

I felt awkward and didn't know what to say. But Linda helped. We asked if the staff was keeping him comfortable. How his kids were doing. If he had visitors yet today. Each time we spoke, he opened his right eye to acknowledge he was listening.

After about five minutes of conversation, which seemed to sap what little energy he had, I walked over to his bedside and said, "Ron, I think we'd better let you get some rest."

"No," he quickly replied. Suddenly, both of his eyes were wide open—for the first and only time during our visit. He reached out and took hold of my hand, almost as though pleading. "If your presence gives me comfort, that's great," he said. "I appreciate your being here."

So Linda and I sat in silence for just another ten minutes, until the medication began to take hold of him. Linda whispered to me that we really should let him sleep and that we needed to say good-bye to him now.

"We're going to let you get some sleep now," I told him.

"OK," he replied, with one eye open.

"Do you mind if I pray for you?"

"Please."

I took his hand in mine, and he held on with a surprisingly tight grip, which he sustained throughout my short prayer. I leaned over the bed and gently spoke the words into his ear. I doubt that even Linda, standing beside me, could hear them. I thanked God for Ron's life, and I asked God to help the nurses and the doctors keep him comfortable.

After I spoke the "Amen," I did something so out of character that I would leave the room a bit embarrassed and wondering where the reflex had come from. I kissed Ron on his forehead. My brothers and I had often kissed our father exactly like that during his bouts with cancer. But he was our father. I hardly knew Ron. Looking back, I find myself wondering if my action was not a mere conditioned reflex but a message from God to Ron.

"Rest well, Ron," I said. And we were gone. He died a week later.

I find it curious that, though I almost decided against visiting Ron because I was so busy, I can't remember what I was working on. I've long since forgotten. But I doubt that I'll ever forget those fifteen minutes with Ron.

Death tends to drive people away. Even doctors make themselves scarce when the end draws near, mistakenly thinking of death as failure instead of a natural part of life on this planet. Many folks die alone, or nearly so.

A Death Watch for Dad

I don't think I could have worked up the courage to go and see Ron had it not been for insights I gained ten months earlier, when I spent the night on a death watch at the hospital bedside of my father.

Dad, at age sixty-eight, had fought non-Hodgkin's lymphoma for twenty years. He did it with a valor and strength of spirit that I marveled at in the early years and later came to think of as an inheritance—a gift to his children that showed us how we can one day face the ultimate adversity. In many ways, Dad struck me as a modern-style knight driving back an invader. Instead of riding a stallion or carrying a sword, Dad straddled a seven-hundred-pound Harley and he toted a chain saw. He loved riding his motorcycle, and he took joy in climbing trees and trimming them for his family and neighbors.

I think his enhanced joy of life came from knowing that he was supposed to have died at age forty-eight, within six months of learning about his disease. In fact, he nearly did die during the first chemotherapy and again fourteen years later during radiation treatment for a malignant tumor that erupted inside his throat. But at sixty-eight, Dad was still sailing the highway on his black, chrome-dressed Harley and climbing sixty-foot trees with his chain saw.

That's when the lymphoma struck a third time, packing Dad's bone marrow and emerging as a lump inside his right temple. In response, Dr. Thomas Budd, an oncologist at the Cleveland Clinic, ordered an unusually toxic mixture of chemotherapy. For one restless week a month, Dad stayed in the hospital as ten bags of brown, cancer-fighting chemicals dripped into his veins.

The day after his third regimen—January 12, 1995—Dad lay parchment white and twenty-four pounds lighter on his living room couch. Remnants of his hair hung limp and long in randomly scattered strands. He was shivering with chills, though triple-layered. He wore the blue-checkered flannel pajamas I had bought him for Christmas. Over that he had wrapped his flannel housecoat. On top Mom had placed a thick afghan knitted in a pattern of three-inch stripes of light and happy colors: white, pastel green, white, soft yellow, white, gentle pink, white, and a checkerboard of all four colors. She nudged the thermostat up to seventy-five degrees.

Dad refused to let Mom call the doctor, for he knew he would be readmitted to the hospital. "If I can get upstairs to the waterbed, I'll be OK," he said.

The waterbed is heated and a toasty place to recover on a frigid winter day. My youngest brother, Darb, a muscular six-foot-one, came to visit in the early afternoon on his way to work. With a strong embrace he helped Dad to his feet, but almost immediately our father collapsed, unconscious. As my brother scooped him up, he thought about how Dad used to hold him. But now the son felt as if *he* were the father holding the child. Darb could have carried Dad upstairs, but he didn't. He said he thought it would have stripped away what remained of our father's dignity.

Early that evening one of my sisters, Louise, came to the house. At Dad's insistence, she and Mom tried again to help Dad up the stairs. They supported him from both sides, grasping him around his waist and pulling his arms tight upon their shoulders. Before they reached the first stair, Dad slipped through their arms and crumbled to the carpet. There, in a heap, he lurched and moaned through a seizure. My sister thought he was dying, and she cried, "No, Dad! No, Dad! No, Dad!"

Unconscious, our father wet himself. When he came to, he began to gag as his stomach tried to empty itself; but there was nothing to empty. Sprawled on the floor, Dad cried.

Mom told him that he would be OK. She washed him with a wet cloth and changed his pajamas. Then she and my sister followed behind him as he crawled back to the couch. They were afraid he would pass out again if he stood.

Louise lives only a few miles away, and she pleaded to spend the night. But Mom told her to go home and take care of her young family: "I'll call you if I need you."

A short time later Mom called my brother Cliff, who had not yet realized how frail Dad was. Mom wanted him to see Dad and to be prepared to let go if it became necessary. Cliff is a big man of more than two hundred pounds. Wearing his heavy winter coat, he's an imposing figure. He came in the house from the back door, into the kitchen. Quietly he walked toward the dining room, took a short step inside, and leaned right so he could peek through the living room entryway and steal a glance at Dad.

Our father was sitting on the floor in front of the couch, his body leaning left and his head cocked back onto one of the seat cushions. Dad was on the floor because it was there—kneeling and with his forehead propped against the couch—that he relieved himself with a portable urinal. He then sat and rested before laboriously climbing back onto the couch.

Cliff retreated to the kitchen and broke into sobs. When he finally ventured into the living room, he sat down on the floor beside Dad. Still wearing his blizzard-proof coat, Cliff put an arm around our father and asked, "Is it OK if I cry?"

Dad gave a single nod. They both wept.

There on the floor, Cliff prayed out loud, asking God to help Dad. When the words were finished Cliff lifted Dad back onto the couch, then sat for a long while in the recliner a couple feet away.

At bedtime, Mom and Dad were alone again, with Mom curled up in the recliner, where she intended to spend the night. But as Dad grew increasingly restless and uncomfortable, she gathered the cushions from the love seat and built a bed on the floor beside the couch. Dad often held Mom's hand as they slept together, and she thought if she could get close enough for him to hold her again he might rest easier.

But Dad wanted more than a warm hand. He wished aloud for his warm bed.

"I can't help you walk up the stairs," Mom said.

"I can crawl," Dad replied.

Mom protested, asking what would happen if he couldn't make it all the way.

"I'd rest."

Dad rolled gently to the floor. On hands and knees he began to crawl. It was ten feet to the living room doorway. There he stopped and lay on the floor to rest. Mom knelt beside him and covered him with the afghan of white and green and yellow and pink. A few minutes later Dad rose and crawled six more feet to the foot of the carpeted staircase. Using the first stair as a pillow, he lay down once again. And again my mother knelt and covered him.

It took him about forty-five minutes to negotiate a distance he could normally cover in a few seconds. But he made it to bed.

He almost died that night. Sometime after midnight he tried to walk to the bathroom, bracing himself against the walls of the hallway. Mom heard him fall, ran to him, then followed him as he crawled back to the bedroom and lay on the floor, unable to climb into bed.

About 1 A.M. on what had become Friday the 13th, my mother called me. She told me what had happened, then asked a question that left me without words, "Where's the dignity?"

"Come home," she said. "I need the whole family here to help me." Mom then called my sister, who drove right over. The two of them pleaded with Dad to let them call the paramedics. He refused until Mom, weeping, placed her forehead on his and whispered, "Please. Do this for me."

Dad didn't want to go to the hospital because he didn't want to die there. Mom promised to bring him home as soon as he was stabilized.

Longtime neighbors, awakened by the siren, looked out

their windows and, seeing a body covered from head to toe on that frozen winter night, feared they had lost their friend.

By the time I arrived at Akron General Medical Center that afternoon, doctors had concluded that a viral infection had attacked Dad when his white blood cells were nearly depleted. The chemotherapy temporarily stops the bone marrow from producing infection-fighting white cells. Dad's struggle to survive was overworking his heart muscle, previously injured in a series of light heart attacks. His condition became so critical that our family divided the days and nights and kept watch over him. For a change, five offspring became an advantage.

My sister Louise stood with me in the hall as we gave Pam, the youngest of the family, time to sit with Dad.

"I know I should thank God for these twenty years," Louise said, "but all I can do is ask for twenty more."

I spent the night with Dad, sitting with my head two feet from his. He lay in the tight curl of an unborn child, yet he looked like a corpse discarded. Skin white and drawn. Face gaunt and misshapen, with the mouth closed on the right and opened a crack at the extreme left. *This is how he will look when he is dead,* I thought.

His irregular breathing through the crack in his mouth sounded inhuman, like the raspy, artificial puffing of a respirator about to fail. I couldn't possibly sleep. During that night, I watched my father. I studied his form. It seemed as flesh, without a spirit. I wondered if he was leaving before my very eyes. And I tried, without success, to remember a time I had told him he had been a good father to me.

We had walked the walk but not talked that kind of talk. Now, I feared, I might never get to speak the words.

From a Harley-riding grandpa who would burst onto the

highway at heavy throttle, he had become in three months a pathetic creature crawling on the floor, a near-corpse clinging to life by the thread of IVs feeding him nourishment, antibiotics, and blood—a man about whom his wife repeatedly asked family and physician, "Where's the dignity?"

In the long hours of the evening, out of the darkness came the memory of a scene I had read many times. It was of Jesus collapsed on the ground. He had crumbled into the dirt while walking to his death. In the twinkling of an eye another thought arose. That thought felt sentient, like a living force that had been sleeping and forgotten but that was abruptly awakened by something outside of me. *There was dignity in the suffering of Jesus*, the thought said.

My response was immediate. *Is there dignity in my father's suffering?*

I began to think about what Dad's suffering had produced. When he collapsed into the arms of his children, in his helplessness he drew from them the one response that Jesus praised above all others: compassionate love. When Dad crawled up the stairs, compassion followed him with an afghan of many colors. When he lay in the hospital, too weak to talk let alone crawl, his entire family descended upon him, and compassion guarded him all hours of the day and night.

There's the dignity.

Lying helpless, my father had the power to draw out of others the trait above all traits. When the first light of morning arrived, Dad woke. Together we watched the white shroud of fog slowly retreat from the hospital courtyard and the first-shift workers scurry out of the cloud as they curled themselves around insulated cups of steaming coffee.

In the silence I tried to speak but twice was overcome by

waves of emotion that dissolved my words even as my lips began to move. On the third try, composed only enough to whisper, I talked the talk. I told Dad he had been a good father.

To the astonishment of everyone in our family, Dad survived the crisis by outlasting the infection. Since then, he has trimmed more trees and ridden his Harley along country highways. He has also fought yet another bout with cancer, taking more chemotherapy, which failed to reduce a tumor in his stomach, and then a new drug that produced a remarkable shrinkage.

Perhaps, I hope, we can have another twenty years. If not, we have today. And we make the most of each one. Though I live eight hundred miles from Dad and Mom, I talk with them each week. We try to visit each other several times a year, sometimes taking vacations together, from picking blueberries in Maine to gathering seashells in Florida. We've even watched country music performers pick and grin in Nashville and Branson.

Dying Well

When it comes time to die, we human beings usually want one thing most of all: we want to be surrounded by friends and family. And if relationships with any of these people have been damaged, we want to mend them. If we don't have this, dying can become torturous.

Patricia Kelley, a hospice nurse and coauthor of *Final Gifts*, a book about what dying people can teach us, told me that some of her patients have clung to life much longer than anyone expected—and they did so because they were waiting for a loved one to arrive. Fear that the friend or family member won't come can actually produce symptoms that suggest the patient is dying in great pain: moaning, agitation, confusion.

Kelley watched that happen to a thirty-nine-year-old man dying of AIDS, waiting for his estranged father to arrive. The dad had severed all ties with his son three years earlier, when the young man broke the news that he was gay and infected with HIV.

As death approached, the young man's mother said she wanted to bring her son home. "The dad didn't want that to happen," Kelley remembers. "The dad said, 'If you bring that kid home here, then I'm leaving.' She did, and he left."

The mom brought her boy home on Friday. "We truly thought he would die over the weekend," Kelley said. "He lived another couple of weeks. And what he was saying was he needed to see his father." The father never came.

But Kelley remembers another patient: a woman in her mid-fifties who was dying of cancer and fighting to stay alive long enough for her family to track down her youngest child, a daughter who had left home as an angry teenager seven years earlier. There had been harsh words between mother and daughter, and the daughter still blamed her mom for driving her away from home and into drugs. But the young woman's brother and sister found her and talked her into coming home.

It was late in the evening when the daughter arrived. By then, the mother was close to death. She had been holding on for this moment alone. "She was too weak to smile," Kelley remembers of the mom. "But there was a smile in her eyes. She mouthed the girl's name."

The daughter sat on her mother's bed, instantly and deeply

moved by the scene engulfing her. In words hushed and tender, she explained that she was old enough now to see that she was to blame for much of the tension between them but that she hadn't been able to bring herself to apologize ... until now.

The two talked throughout the night. It was a time of amazement and deep healing, says Kelley. Early the next morning the mother died in peace, surrounded by her family.

When I Die

I deeply admired the late astronomer Carl Sagan, who rhapsodized about a universe with "billions and billions" of stars. With his contagious enthusiasm and his gift for translating complex science into everyday language, he inspired millions and millions to turn their eyes to the wondrous and incomprehensible creation.

At age sixty-two, in 1996, he died of pneumonia after a two-year battle with the rare bone marrow disease myelodysplasia. Nine months earlier, while lying in bed at Fred Hutchinson Cancer Research Center, he wrote an article titled "In the Valley of the Shadow." As much as I admired Sagan and shared his love of space exploration, I don't want to die as he said he would die. Without hope.

"I would love to believe that when I die I will live again," he wrote, "that some thinking, feeling, remembering part of me will continue. But as much as I want to believe that, and despite the ancient and worldwide cultural traditions that assert an afterlife, I know of nothing to suggest that it is more than wishful thinking."

Sagan said this perspective may have given him extra motivation to stay alive and to be grateful every day for the magnificent opportunity that life provides. Near his shaving mirror, so he could see it every morning, Sagan kept a framed postcard. On the back was penciled a message to James Day of Swansea Valley, Wales. It read:

Dear Friend,

Just a line to show that I am alive & kicking and going grand. It's a treat.

Yours,
WJR

The initials were of William John Rogers. On the front of the postcard was a color photo of a sleek, four-stack steamer captioned "White Star Liner *Titanic*." The postmark was stamped the day before the ship went down, claiming more than fifteen hundred lives, including that of William Rogers. "I display the postcard for a reason," Sagan wrote. "We know that 'going grand' can be the most temporary and illusory state."

Sagan's zeal for life, fueled by his keen awareness that human life is fleeting, is worthy of emulation. But I can't understand why he thought of the afterlife as only a forlorn hope and of people who believe in the afterlife and God as "feeble souls." He explained his thoughts in the article's closing words, which he borrowed from Albert Einstein:

"I cannot conceive of a god who rewards and punishes his creatures or has a will of the kind that we experience in ourselves. Neither can I—nor would I want to—conceive of an individual that survives his physical death. Let feeble souls, from fear or absurd egotism, cherish such thoughts. I am satisfied with the mystery of the eternity of life and a glimpse of the marvelous structure of the existing world, together with the devoted striving to comprehend a portion, be it ever so tiny, of the Reason that manifests itself in nature."

How could such great minds search the depths of creation, one studying the minute atom and another exploring the vast universe, and not see evidence of the Creator? And how could they describe the design of creation as one of Reason without perceiving that there's an intelligence behind that Reason?

The apostle Paul expressed the paradox well: "God in his wisdom saw to it that the world would never find him through human wisdom" (1 Corinthians 1:21, *New Living Translation*).

Sagan and Einstein aren't the only brilliant human beings who've argued that life ends with our last breath. The planet is filled with realists, as they might like to be called. Some of these people have recently been trying to figure out how best to explain death to children.

Psychiatrists have discovered that children at age six are just beginning to understand the four key characteristics of death: it has a cause, involves the end of bodily function, is irreversible, and is universal. Some psychiatrists recommend that, for children who can't handle these ideas, it's OK to console them with the fantasy that someday researchers may invent a pill that will let us live forever. In fact, biologists have found eight genes that, when manipulated, can quadruple the life span of the roundworm, a creature much closer to humans genetically than their appearance suggests.

Yet my instinct doesn't get excited by molecular biologists who argue that, if the bristlecone pine lives for five thousand years, why can't we? My gut also tells me that the scholars who teach immortality as a myth are dead wrong. Instead, I find myself drawn to ideas that the brilliant of our world criticize as feeble and foolish. Not only because of the Bible or my personal religious experiences, but it is because of my innate sense of immortality that I gravitate to the simpleminded, six-and-under crowd. When four-year-old Cecilia Cichan survived the crash of Northwest Airlines Flight 255 in Detroit on August 16, 1987, and was told that her parents and brother had died and that she would never see them again, she asked what "never again" meant.

Could it possibly be that Einstein, Sagan, and an intimidating crowd of the brilliant are wrong? That a four-year-old got it right? That "never again" is meaningless? That spiritual beings are meant to live forever with their Creator?

Over the years, I've interviewed many people who have returned from the brink of death and brought back astonishing stories of a journey's start into an afterlife that shimmers with light and is graced with familiar faces. I've also talked with physicians who believe the stories, convinced by patients' accurate descriptions of procedures and instrument readings that the patients could not have known had their spirits not left their bodies.

Like you, perhaps, I wonder if these are another of God's efforts to reach out to a skeptical, unbelieving world. Or maybe God intends them for believers, to comfort and reassure us in the face of our greatest fear: oblivion, nothingness.

God does reassure. Sometimes in mysterious, marvelous ways. When my sixty-five-year-old Grandpap was dying of prostate cancer, he asked his wife if she would take him out of the hospital so he could die at home. He was in terrible pain, which doctors were unsuccessfully trying to control with morphine. The hospital staff recommended against releasing Grandpap, but he went home anyhow.

"As soon as we got him home, a peace went over him," my Uncle Henry remembers. "He was calm, clearheaded. Good shape."

That was on Thursday. Friday was a good day too. And so was Saturday, until around 11:00 at night, when the convulsions began. These continued all through Sunday. "I hear angels singing," he told his wife during that traumatic weekend.

About daybreak on Monday, it became clear that Grandpap was near death. Henry, Grandpap's youngest son, began reading from the Twenty-third Psalm: "The Lord is my shepherd; I shall not want. He maketh me to lie down in green pastures: he leadeth me beside the still waters. He restoreth my soul" (v.v. 1-3a *King James Version*). After Grandpap drew his last breath, Henry sat looking at his father. A palpable, holy presence filled the room. Suddenly, my uncle saw something so astonishing, so unbelievable, that he has told only a few people in the three-and-a-half decades since it happened.

"I saw a vapor of his body asleep; it looked like a vapor, a mist," my uncle said. "It just slowly lifted up out of him." Dumbfounded, Henry watched as the translucent image slowly rose some three to four feet before disappearing.

I asked my uncle if he was terrified.

"It never scared me the least bit. It sure felt good to me. I mean, I wasn't happy, but I knew that everything was all right."

This took place on August 3, 1964, long before related accounts of near-death experiences began making headlines, with the publication of Raymond Moody's best-selling book *Life After Life* in 1975.

Noted Christian physician Paul Brand also testifies of a mystifying reassurance about the afterlife. Brand is a renowned hand surgeon, leprosy specialist, and coauthor of the best-sellers *Fearfully and Wonderfully Made* and *In His Image*. About twenty years ago, he had a patient named Rose Kato, who lay tied to the railings of her hospital bed. She would be dead in a few hours, but for the moment she was fighting to break loose.

This Hawaiian woman was more than a patient to Brand; she was his friend. In years past, with her hands paralyzed by advanced leprosy and frozen at the joints, she had managed to teach his children the hula. But now her kidneys had failed, and Brand had transferred her from the leprosy hospital at Carville, Louisiana, to General Hospital in Baton Rouge. An infection in her arm forced the hospital staff to start dialysis in her peritoneum. But the dialysis fluid in her abdomen quickly became infected. "With a gross peritonitis, it was very clear that she was beyond our help," Brand told me.

"My wife and I went to visit her in the hospital, with a tape from the people in the church—they taped the Sunday morning choir," Brand recalled. "We found her in the intensive care with tubes everywhere, down her mouth and into her stomach, tubes for oxygen into her nose, and tubes into her veins." Her arms were restrained because she had been pulling out the tubes.

"She couldn't say a word because of the tubes in her mouth," Brand said, "but it was obvious she wanted to talk." Brand ordered the restraints and tubes removed. Kato, who should have been suffering intense pain in the abdomen, showed no sign of discomfort.

"She sat up in bed, just beaming!" Brand said, his voice suddenly beginning to beam, too, as he recounted the experience for me.

"Isn't it wonderful!" Kato said. "Can't you see him?"

"I said, 'Rose, who should I be seeing?'"

"It's Jesus! He's come for me! There he is! Can't you see him? He's standing at the end of the bed just waiting for me! And you people are trying to hold me back!"

Brand and his wife wept. "We just embraced her, and assured her that Jesus had come for her and that she would be seeing him soon, in Glory.... She died that night in great peace."

Did Kato *really* see Jesus? "I have no doubt," Brand said. "She clearly recognized the presence of Jesus Christ in a human form in her room."

It's not out of "fear or absurd egotism," as Einstein proposed, that I embrace the hope of immortality. I do so for many reasons, beginning with the knowledge of God's power evidenced in creation and continuing with the resurrection of Jesus, the teachings of Scripture, the experiences of saints throughout the ages, and my own spiritual experiences as well as those of others I know and trust.

A Celestial Sunset

If I had the *Titanic* postcard from WJR, I might put it beside my mirror, too, just as Carl Sagan did. It would remind me to cherish the present moments. But I think I'd place beside it the picture of a southern Florida sunset. It would remind me of the immortal moments ahead. For it was on a summer evening in 1997, along the shores of Fort Myers Beach, that I sensed the majesty of heaven.

I was on vacation with my family, and I had received a call

that a fellow church member and longtime friend of mine had died—a gentle spirit and thoughtful writer named Ivan Beals. A few nights later, at about 8:15, I took a solitary walk along the beach. I wasn't thinking about Ivan as the walk began, but that was soon to change.

Storms had drenched the coastline off and on throughout the day, but now enormous billowy clouds trailing the final storm burst into color: hues of red, orange, yellow, gold, and silver. One massive, bulging mountain of a cloud hovered above the sea before me, leaving just a tiny crack of sky below, through which I could watch the sun begin slipping into the water. But high above, at the craggy top of the cloud mountain, a fan of heavenly rays shot up and out in all directions. This radiance painted the top line of the cloud silver, and for the first time I realized where the poet got the phrase "There's a silver lining behind every cloud." I had never seen it before.

I felt as if I were watching more than a masterfully choreographed sunset. No, this was more like what I experience when I'm driving at night toward a big city. Long before I reach the city I catch sight of its glow in the sky. This Florida sunset appeared like a glow of the celestial city ahead: "The city does not need the sun or the moon to shine on it, for the glory of God gives it light" (Revelation 21:23).

For a few short moments, I felt as if this single shimmering mountain of cloud was the only obstacle hiding from my sight all the glory and majesty of heaven. Suddenly, my spiritual home became as real to me as the earth on which I was standing. As real as distant cities bustling beneath the glow of the night sky.

All around me, sunset beach walkers stopped to stare into

the sky. Some pointed their cameras upward, as though they could possibly capture the beauty. There on the shoreline, with all action frozen into slow motion, I found myself picturing righteous souls scurrying about in heaven, doing whatever joyful activities God has planned for them. And smiling—right there on the beach—I envisioned my friend Ivan caught up amid this scurrying in the city of light.

As the last flicker of sun dipped into the gulf, I knew I should make a wish. I had taught my children to do as much during sunsets past.

But I could think of nothing I wanted. For I was filled with the wonder and glory of the moment.